∼SO YOU THINK YOU'RE **FAT?**∼

SO YOU ~THINK~ YOU'RE FAT?

All About Obesity, Anorexia Nervosa, Bulimia Nervosa, and Other Eating Disorders

Dr. Alvin & Virginia B. Silverstein
with Robert Silverstein

HarperCollins*Publishers*

SO YOU THINK YOU'RE FAT
Copyright © 1991 by Alvin Silverstein,
Virginia B. Silverstein, and Robert A. Silverstein
All rights reserved. No part of this book may be
used or reproduced in any manner whatsoever without
written permission except in the case of brief quotations
embodied in critical articles and reviews. Printed in
the United States of America. For information address
HarperCollins Children's Books, a division of
HarperCollins Publishers, 10 East 53rd Street,
New York, NY 10022.
Typography by Elynn Cohen
1 2 3 4 5 6 7 8 9 10
First Edition

Library of Congress Cataloging-in-Publication Data
Silverstein, Alvin.
  So you think you're fat / Alvin, Virginia, and Robert Silverstein.
    p.   cm.
  Summary: Explains the nature, causes, and effects of common eating
disorders, including anorexia nervosa and bulimia.
  ISBN 0-06-021641-7. — ISBN 0-06-021642-5 (lib. bdg.)
  1. Eating disorders—Juvenile literature.   2. Obesity—
Psychological aspects—Juvenile literature.   [1. Eating disorders.
2. Obesity.]   I. Silverstein, Virginia B.   II. Silverstein, Robert A.
III. Title.
RC552.E18S55   1991   90-40761
616.85′26—dc20   CIP
                                                          AC

CONTENTS

1 The Pound Plague 1

2 What's the Right Weight? 7

3 Body Image 15

4 Dangers of Obesity 30

5 Where the Food Goes 39

6 Why Do People Get Fat? 54

7 Addicted to Food? 79

8 Diet Mania 92

9 Making a Diet Work 104

10 Burn It Off 124

11 Getting Help 141

12 More Weight-Loss Aids 156

13 Anorexia Nervosa 175

14 Bulimia Nervosa 189

15 Maintaining the Right Weight
   for *You* 203

Further Reading 207

Index 209

~SO YOU THINK YOU'RE **FAT?**~

THE POUND PLAGUE

DO YOU THINK you weigh too much? If so, you are right in style. Most Americans today are so weight conscious that their concern with excess pounds seems like an obsession. Walk into any supermarket or flip through the ads in a magazine, and you'll see "diet/lite" foods and beverages on display. Check the list of current best-sellers, and you're almost sure to find at least one diet book. Your family has probably received dozens of fliers in the mail, each selling some "guaranteed" diet plan. Diet drinks and foods, weight-loss centers, and other aids to losing weight are now more than a thirty-*billion*-dollar-a-year industry!

Obesity, or in more everyday terms overweight,

is a widespread problem these days. Health experts estimate that from a fifth to a quarter of all Americans are substantially overweight—20 percent or more above the number of pounds they should weigh. According to recent reports, the fitness fads of the eighties, with their emphasis on exercise programs and healthier eating styles, have failed to make a dent in the pound problem. Long-term studies of thousands of people in Minnesota and Rhode Island suggest that Americans are actually getting fatter. During the eighties, women gained an average of six to seven pounds, and men put on three to four pounds.

Most people who worry about their weight are concerned mainly with their appearance, but obesity can contribute to some real health problems. Those who carry around extra pounds are more likely to come down with serious illnesses such as heart disease, cancer, diabetes, and gall bladder disease. They tend to die earlier than thinner people.

Fat people also suffer from prejudice. People may think they are lazy and have no willpower. Thin people are seen as more attractive, and fat people have a more difficult time getting jobs and making new friends. Prejudice against the overweight is just as real—and damaging—as racial or religious prejudice.

Many health experts believe that some—perhaps even most—of the people who think they are fat are really worrying needlessly. It seems that worrying about weight is a far more widespread epidemic in America today than obesity itself. In one recent survey, for example, 90 percent of the people polled said they weigh too much, and more than a third said they would like to lose at least fifteen pounds. That's quite a difference from the estimates that 20 to 25 percent of the population are really obese. Actually, even the experts don't all agree on what the "right weight" is for good health, and popular views of the "ideal figure" have varied greatly over the years.

Why are some people fat and others thin? Why is it so difficult to lose those extra pounds? And once lost, why do they seem to creep back on again, time after time? If people *want* to lose weight, why do they find it so difficult to become thin and stay that way?

Scientists have a number of theories as to why two people who eat the same meals will put on weight differently. Doctors have devised many plans and schemes to lose weight. They may be successful for a while, but few continue to work over a span of years. Most people seem to gain those pounds back again.

Some people actually seem to be addicted to eating more food than they really need.

Others—typically girls or young women— seem to develop a kind of addiction to *losing* weight. They are so obsessed with getting thin that just the thought of eating food is upsetting. And yet, the thinner they get, the more convinced they are that they are fat. How could this be possible when all their friends tell them they are just skin and bones? They may diet so much that they starve to death! These people suffer from an eating disorder called *anorexia nervosa*.

Meanwhile, some people (again, mostly young women) go on food binges, gobbling down pounds of cakes or pizzas or other tasty treats at one sitting. Then they feel so guilty that they sneak off to the bathroom and make themselves vomit. They may do this so often that they literally burn their insides with the acid digestive juices and suffer constant pain. Still, they continue. The medical name for their condition is *bulimia nervosa*. Experts estimate that one in eight teenage girls suffers from a serious eating disorder.

Eating is an important part of our lives. For many Americans, though, it has become a central part, and thinking about food (or about the effects of eating on appearance and fitness) has become much too important. Under the pressures of the ideal images our society presents, the constant temptations that surround us, and the frustrations of daily life, eating can get out of hand.

Recovering alcoholics or former drug addicts are advised never to take a drink or use drugs again. But people for whom food has become an addiction can't use that kind of solution. Eating is a necessity—we literally can't live without food.

So what should you do if you are fat?—or if you *think* you are fat?

You won't find any surefire diets or miracle weight-loss programs in the pages that follow—they don't exist. What you will find is the kind of background information you need to evaluate those miracle claims and to work out a sane and balanced style of eating that is right for *you*. You'll learn more about what eating disorders are, and what researchers are finding out about their causes and how to control them. You will also learn about diet, nutrition, and what the body does with the foods we eat; about the consequences of over- and undereating; and about people's helpful and harmful attitudes toward weight. This is the kind of information you need to help you think more intelligently about your own eating habits, to decide whether you have a weight problem, and to work toward solving it if you do.

WHAT'S THE RIGHT WEIGHT?

AMERICANS ARE AMONG the fattest people in the world. Obesity is also a major health problem in Europe, especially in the USSR. Among some tribes of South American Indians, an estimated 50 percent of the population is overweight. The problem affects all ages; in the United States, even children are fatter today than ever before, with one out of four weighing 20 percent or more above their ideal weight.

Actually, that is the medical definition of *obese*—weighing 20 percent or more above one's ideal weight. As many as sixty million Americans fit into that category. According to Dr. Ernst Drenick at the UCLA School of Medicine, "obesity is a disease." Even being ten pounds overweight can increase a person's chances of becoming ill and perhaps shorten his or her life. An estimated thirty-three million of the obese are what specialists call *significantly obese*, weighing 30 percent more than they should. Obesity has greatly increased the health risks for these people, making them nearly twice as likely to develop a life-shortening illness. About six million Americans are more than one hundred pounds overweight—weighing up to twice as much as they should. These unfortunate people are called *morbidly obese*, and their health risks are even greater.

Americans are all too conscious of their weight. Polls have estimated that about seventy million Americans are dieting right now, and over half the people in the United States have been on a diet in the past five years. Yet only a quarter of the population fits the medical definition of obesity, which means that many of the people who are dieting are really only a little overweight—or perhaps not even overweight at all.

Just what is the "right weight"? How do doctors determine the "ideal" that is the standard for defining obesity, and why is there such a difference between the medical and the popular views?

Normal weights are usually given in charts or tables such as those compiled by the Metropolitan Life Insurance Company. A range of normal weights is given for each height. (That seems sensible—a person who is six feet tall would naturally weigh more than a five-footer.) Normal weights depend on a person's sex: A woman's body build is quite different from a man's, and her weight is distributed differently. Body builds also differ: Some people have broad frames with thick, heavy bones, while others are built on a narrower plan, with thinner, lighter bones. Two people of the same height, with different body builds, could have quite different weights and still be perfectly healthy. (That is why height-weight tables give ranges, rather than a single number for each height.) Age is still another important factor: People tend to gain weight as they get older. For instance, a man of twenty who is 5'10" tall and weighs 150 pounds would be within the range of normal weight. When he reaches the age of sixty, he might weigh 205 pounds and still be considered normal by some experts, even though his height hasn't changed.

The "normal" weight ranges are based on surveys of large numbers of healthy people. There is some disagreement among the experts about whether they are really the best standards for good health. In 1983, for example, when Metropolitan Life came out with a revision of its tables of "desirable" weights, the numbers for each height were several pounds higher than they had been in the 1959 tables. The American Heart Association complained that the new weights were too high to be healthy. Some researchers, such as Reubin Andres of the National Institute on Aging, said that the tables did not take the normal age changes into account—so the values given by the Metropolitan Life tables were too high for young adults, just about right for people in their early forties, and too low for the middle-aged and elderly.

The height-weight tables can be misleading in other ways, too. The increased health risks that obesity brings are not really due to the extra *weight*, but rather to the extra *fat* the obese person is carrying around. A bodybuilder could be 25 percent or more "overweight," judging by the typical height-weight tables, yet still be perfectly healthy. The extra weight is muscle, not fat. Doctors call this muscle *lean body mass.* As people get older, they lose this lean body mass and replace it with fat tissue.

The amount of water the body has stored away also influences a person's weight. A baseball pitcher can lose ten pounds during a game on a hot summer day—mainly from the water he has lost by sweating. Many women regularly gain several pounds each month around the time of their menstrual period, when the body is retaining water, and then lose the extra pounds a few days later when the water is flushed away.

So when you step on a scale, you really can't be sure whether the weight you have just gained or lost is body fat, muscle, or water.

Today, athletes are mostly concerned with how much body fat they have. They measure it regularly, to test how well their fitness program is getting along. But some doctors feel that ordinary people should be getting body-fat tests, too. These tests should be given frequently, along with blood tests and tests for cholesterol and triglycerides (a type of fat). Each can tell a great deal about a person's health.

A number of tests have been developed to find

out just how fat a person actually is.

In the *hydrostatic weighing test*, the person is lowered into a tank of water. The person's body displaces water, and the water level in the tank rises. The amount it rises, combined with the values of the person's height and weight, can be used to calculate the proportions of muscle and fat in the body. (Muscle tissue is heavier than fat, so a sample of muscle would displace more water than a fat sample of the same volume.)

Another method uses special instruments called *skinfold calipers*. These are cliplike devices that are attached to layers of fat over various parts of the body, usually on the abdomen, upper back, thighs, and triceps (a muscle in the arm).

Another test uses *ultrasound*. By passing very-high-frequency sound waves through the skin, doctors can measure how much fat is below.

In the *electrical impedence test*, electrodes are attached to various parts of the body. Fat and muscle conduct electricity in different amounts. (The water in muscle tissue makes it a better conductor than fat.) By reading the meter, a doctor can tell how much fat or muscle is present in various parts of the body.

A new device, the *Fitness & Body Fat Analyzer*, shines infrared light on various parts of the body. Fat, water, and protein each absorb these light waves differently. By measuring how the tissue below the skin reacts, the doctor can tell how much of each is present. The simple hand-held device gives a reading in less than ten seconds and is now being used in hospitals, health clubs, and doctors' offices. There is also a less-expensive version for use at home.

Some doctors feel that a normal male should have a body fat level in the range of 12 to 18 percent. (In other words, somewhere between 12 to 18 percent of the entire weight should be fat tissue.) The normal range for females is somewhat higher, from 18 to 24 percent fat. (Women's bodies typically carry more fat than men's, apparently to provide food for the growth of a baby if the woman should become pregnant.) Athletes are leaner. Doctors who specialize in sports medicine feel that 8 to 14 percent body fat is fine for male athletes, and 14 to 20 percent for females.

Most of the laboratory tests for measuring body fat are very time-consuming and expensive, and even the home version of the Fitness & Body Fat

Analyzer costs a few hundred dollars. But there is a simple and convenient way to get a rough estimate of your "fatness" by calculating your *body mass index (BMI)*. Just weigh yourself, without clothes or shoes, and if your scale measures in pounds, divide the number of pounds by 2.2 to convert it to kilograms. (This is your body mass.) Now measure your height (without shoes)—if you measured in inches, divide by 39.4 to convert it to meters. Square the height (multiply the number of meters by itself) and divide the answer into your body mass to get the BMI. For men, the desirable BMI range is 22 to 24. Men with a BMI over 28.5 are obese. For women the desirable range is 21 to 23, with values over 27.5 considered obese.

BODY IMAGE

MANY EXPERTS BELIEVE that Americans, particularly females, are fixated on fat—we suffer from "fat phobia." In survey after survey, between 50 and 90 percent of American women and girls say they are overweight. Even kindergartners are worried about their weight.

The "fat phobics" aren't just worrying; they're doing something about it. One study found that 89 percent of seventeen-year-old girls were on a diet, and almost 50 percent of the nine-year-olds surveyed were dieting, too. Some people are so concerned about food, it begins to control their lives. Nearly 20 percent of American college women suffer from eating disorders like anorexia nervosa and bulimia nervosa.

It's true that obesity is a serious health problem in America, and one that seems to be getting more widespread. But most of the people who are concerned about their weight shouldn't be. In one study, for example, 58 percent of girls aged five to seventeen thought they were overweight, when in fact only 17 percent were! In another study, 50 percent of college women and 13 percent of college men thought they were too fat, but only 10 percent were. In a study conducted by psychologist Susan C. Wooley, 82 percent of normal-weight women who were polled thought they were overweight, and 45 percent of *underweight* women also thought they weighed too much.

Something strange seems to happen to people's ability to judge size when it applies to their own bodies rather than to objects. In a psychological study, women did quite well when they were asked to estimate the size of a box by moving two points on a bar closer or farther apart. But when they were asked to estimate the size of their chest, waist, and hips in the same way, they made all three measurements too large. The women in this study who said they were happiest with their weight were actually ten pounds below the average for their height!

Those who were really at the right weight said they would feel better if they lost about eight pounds.

Ideals of Beauty

Why do people think they're fat when they really aren't? Psychologists say we are conditioned to believe that thin is beautiful through television shows, commercials, and movies. The media give us the idea that the way a person looks defines the kind of person he or she is. "Thin is in," and "attractive people are happier, more popular, and more successful" are the underlying messages we receive. Even in school the most popular kids are the most physically attractive. Whoever heard of a fat Homecoming Queen? Or a fat cheerleader? Female models are thin and agile, and male models are muscular and fit. Movie and television stars are usually attractive and thin. That is often an illusion, though. In real life those same actors, actresses, and models may look rather ordinary. Makeup, lighting, camera angles, and other tricks can hide imperfections and add glamor.

Not all societies think that thin is beautiful. In

most of the world and through most of history, the "ideal" figure was quite a bit plumper than it is now. A man with a thick waistline and a bulging belly looked solid and prosperous, and plumpness was prized in women, too. The underlying message in those days was that fat people were successful and rich enough to afford all the food they wanted to eat.

There are some solid survival reasons why people of the past prized fatness. In ancient times in the Sahara, for example, obese women were much more desirable, and fatness was a sign of wealth. Famine could happen at any time in the Sahara Desert, and an obese women could still bear a child during hard times and continue nursing it for a year or more, drawing on the excess "food" stored in her body. For this reason new brides were traditionally given excessive amounts of camel's milk to plump them up. This practice is still carried on, thousands of years later, in that area of the world.

Even in America, a full-figured woman has been the ideal throughout history, up to a couple of generations ago. A major change came in the 1920s, when the women's movement won voting rights and women began to take a more active role in life outside the home. Researcher Brett Silverstein of the City College of New York points out that in the twenties there was an exercise fad and a widespread outbreak of eating disorders, just as there is today.

The Depression of the thirties brought a return to more traditional views, but by the 1960s, thinness again became the beauty ideal. It was around that time that doctors' reports about the dangers of obesity started to make headlines. People became more weight conscious, realizing that those extra pounds could harm their health and shorten their lives.

The sixties also brought a peak in the women's movement. Some psychologists believe that as women had to compete with men in the workplace, they became more masculine in appearance. These women believed that men—and other women, too—did not take women with lots of curves seriously.

Being attractive to members of the opposite sex is still a strong motivation for most people to try to be as beautiful as possible. But there seem to be some misunderstandings about what the opposite sex really wants. In a study conducted at

the University of Pennsylvania by psychologists
Paul Rozin and April Fallon, college men and
women were shown two series of silhouettes,
male and female, each going from very thin to
very fat. The women usually pointed to a rather
slim silhouette as the female ideal and indicated a
heavier one when asked which matched their own
bodies. They thought that men regard the slim
female figure as ideal, but when men were shown
the same series of female silhouettes, they chose a
more rounded figure. The men typically had a
more realistic idea of which male silhouette best
matched their own body build, but they thought
that women desire a heavier figure than they really do. In general, though, the men were more
satisfied with their own bodies than the women
were.

Many psychologists believe that entirely too
much emphasis is now being placed on weight.
They are very much against the diet craze; they
view the exercise fad that has swept the nation in
recent years as a positive sign, but they feel that
people need to be more accepting of themselves as
they are—no matter how hard we try, we'll never
be perfect.

Self-image

People who become food obsessed and fall prey to eating disorders like anorexia nervosa, bulimia, and overeating, generally have low *self-esteem*—they do not have a high opinion of their own worth and feel that others do not value them, either. Our *body image* (how we see ourselves and how satisfied we are with what we see) is a very important part of our *self-image* (our sense of identity, or who we are), and it greatly affects our self-esteem. People who are unhappy about the way they look have low self-esteem, and they don't really like themselves. They overlook their good points, such as intelligence or skills, and focus on their physical imperfections. Their *self-perception* (how they think others see them) can also be quite distorted, and they think that others focus only on these imperfections as well.

People who accept the way they look (even if it isn't perfect) and like the way they are have high self-esteem. They allow themselves to take credit for their accomplishments and aren't devastated when they fail at things in life but only try harder next time. Such people rarely fall into the traps that lead to obsessions with food and eating disorders.

Some psychologists believe that people form their self-image during adolescence, and no matter what changes they go through in later life, they always think of themselves in this way. So a fat person who has lost weight may still see him- or herself as a fat person, who just happens to be thinner now. (Actually, there may be some truth to that view, based on some quirks of body physiology, as we shall see later.)

Adolescence is a hard time for many, because an adolescent's body is going through dramatic changes. Teen problems like peer pressure, moving into larger schools, and being caught between being a child and an adult can add to the uncertainty and stress. To an adolescent, looks can be very important in building enough self-esteem to be popular, or just to fit in. But some teens base their entire self-esteem on their body image. Their self-perception may be distorted—and a negative self-image reinforced—when they compare themselves to movie stars and other adult ideals, whose body proportions are quite different from their still-developing adolescent contours.

For adolescents, who desperately want to fit in and be accepted, being fat in a society that says thin is beautiful is not very good for building self-esteem. People are all too likely to make surface judgments—they may look at a fat person and see nothing but an appearance that does not match the current idea of beauty, not the good qualities that may be inside. Fat people often regard themselves this way, too.

Although men generally tend to be more satisfied with their weight than women are, the negative attitudes toward fat can be distressing to both sexes. A study published in 1988, for example, found that men also suffer a lack of self-esteem when they feel too fat or too skinny, although they do not talk about it as much as women do.

The negative views of fat people are formed very early. A study reported in 1983 showed that two- to five-year-old children overwhelmingly preferred thin dolls to fat dolls. In another study, both children and parents ranked fat children below those in wheelchairs, those with disfigured faces, and children with missing limbs. Children quickly learn to apply adjectives like "ugly," "dumb," "lazy," and "sloppy" to fat kids.

Kids often tease other kids, and fat children are the biggest targets for teasing. Some overweight children become the "class clowns," trying to be funny so that the other kids will laugh at their jokes, not at *them*. Others become withdrawn and try to be noticed as little as possible. But people still notice them, and adults may say things that can hurt an overweight child, without realizing they've said anything wrong. (A comment like "What a shame—she has such a pretty face" may be kindly meant, but it hurts all the same.) Parents of fat kids can say and do things that give their children the impression they are ashamed of them. One study found that many parents, even fat parents, often do not include pictures of their fat children in photo albums.

Fat kids are usually the last ones chosen for teams in gym class. They are often outcasts from other groups and activities as well—sometimes by their own choice, sometimes just because they aren't popular. When fat kids grow up, they often find many of the same attitudes in adults.

Studies since the 1960s have found that looks play a big role in who does better in school and who gets the jobs in the business world. One study even found that "good-looking" criminals are less likely to be caught, and when they are they receive shorter sentences.

According to another study, overweight people who are unemployed spend an average of five weeks longer finding a job than thinner unemployed people. Other studies have concluded that overweight men and women, but especially women, are not promoted as often and earn less than thinner people. Several discrimination cases have been won by employees who were fired or were not hired because of their weight. In these cases the judges ruled that unless the employer can prove that a person's weight will interfere with job performance, weight cannot be used as a determining factor for employment. A 1989 ruling in New Jersey declared obesity a handicap under the New Jersey Law Against Discrimination, and thus made obese people eligible for protection under the law.

Changing Attitudes

Recently, studies and polls have found that America's beauty ideals are changing. Thin is no longer quite so "in." Models no longer have that anorexic look—it's now in fashion to have womanly curves. At the Ford Modeling Agency, for example, models are an average five to ten pounds heavier than those of ten years ago. The beanstalk look was fashionable before, but now models and actresses are going for a well-fed, fit look, because people's perceptions of what is healthy have changed. Katie Ford, creative director of the Ford Agency, says this new idea of healthy "isn't just thin, but being in shape."

Anthea Disney, editor of *Self* magazine, believes that baby boomers who have grown up are responsible for the change in society's perception of the "ideal-looking woman." When baby-boomer women were in their twenties, they had to compete against men to get jobs and establish careers, so a "mean and lean" look seemed more masculine. Now that many baby boomers are having children, it's okay to have feminine curves.

Some pyschologists believe there has been only a partial change in attitude, with the "fit and muscular" look replacing thinness as the ideal for successful competition in the working world. They point to the fact that nearly three times as many

women with college degrees prefer the fit look,
compared to women without college degrees, and
rich women prefer "thin and fit" much more than
poor women. But others note that the muscular
trend still allows women to have womanly curves
as well—actresses Kathleen Turner and Cybill
Shepherd, for example, are fit but still have traditional "womanly" figures.

A recent Gallup poll that noted this change in
American tastes revealed that despite the recent
changes in ideal images, we still don't know what
the opposite sex wants. While most women think
they have average "soft" bodies, they want to
have average muscular bodies. They believe, however, that men prefer thin, soft bodies. The poll
found that men prefer average soft-bodied
women over muscular ones. While men are not as
weight conscious, they also would like to be
more muscular, and have broader shoulders and
chests. According to the poll, though, women
think men with average chest and shoulder size
are just fine.

The new trend is encouraging to many psychologists, because a fit look is much more attain-
able and healthy than the ultrathin look that has

been in fashion. Many believe, however, that we need to do more than just substitute one ideal of what's beautiful for another. **We need to broaden our ideals of what is beautiful and become more accepting of ourselves and others when that ideal is not met.**

While the fit look is sweeping the nation, other barriers that have psychologically hurt overweight people are being torn down. Realizing that one out of three American women wears size 16 or larger (size 8 used to be the standard size for models; now 10 is acceptable), the fashion-industry market has greatly changed. Large-size specialty shops are popping up everywhere, and they carry lines of glamorous large-size designer clothes. Plus-size models are becoming more popular to show off the attractive new clothes, and they are helping to banish the myth that big can't be beautiful. There is even a monthly magazine for larger women called *Big Beautiful Woman.*

Popular television characters like Roseanne Barr, whose sitcom has been a hit since it first appeared at the end of the eighties, are also helping to change some of the feelings and prejudices that many people have toward overweight people. They are providing positive role models for young people and may promote greater tolerance and understanding of those with weight problems.

DANGERS
OF OBESITY

OBESITY CAN BE a real burden, a handicap in many different ways. From ads for diet foods and fitness programs to people's disapproving stares and rude remarks, our modern world keeps sending the message that fatness is bad. There is also the literal, physical burden of carrying around more pounds than the body's bones and muscles were built to handle. The extra weight puts a strain on other systems, too, especially the heart and blood vessels.

Statistics show that those who are overweight do not live as long as thinner people. While they do live, they suffer from many more diseases and health complications as well. So many people die from ailments caused or made worse by being overweight that obesity ranks second to smoking in causing deaths that people could have avoided by changing their life-style.

The Major Killers

The leading cause of death in this country is heart disease, and being overweight greatly increases the chances of suffering a heart attack.

A heart attack can occur when blood vessels that supply oxygen and nutrients to the heart muscle are blocked. These blood vessels are called coronary arteries; doctors call a blockage of these vital blood vessels a coronary occlusion.

There are three coronary arteries. Each feeds a different part of the heart. When one of these arteries is blocked by a blood clot, the heart cells it supplied are starved and begin to die within hours.

High levels of cholesterol in the blood are found to lead to a narrowing of the coronary arteries and thus to heart attacks. Fat people have a much higher than normal level of cholesterol in their blood. Triglyceride levels are also much higher in fat people; this, too, can lead to heart attacks.

High blood pressure causes the heart to work much harder than it normally does. Scientists have also found evidence that high blood pressure causes heart blockages to occur more often. And—you guessed it: Obese people, especially young adults who are overweight, have higher blood pressure than thinner people.

This same high blood pressure leads to many other problems in the body. It damages the kidneys, the liver, the lungs, and many other parts of the body. So fat people suffer and die from the breakdown of these vital body organs.

Each year over one hundred thousand people die from strokes. These are the result of a sudden mishap in one of the blood vessels in the brain. Perhaps a fat-clogged artery becomes blocked, preventing the blood from flowing on; or the blood-vessel wall may tear, allowing blood to leak out instead of flowing through its normal channels. In either case, the supply of oxygen and nutrients to the brain cells "downstream" of the problem is cut off. Brain cells are very delicate; just a few minutes without oxygen can kill them. So when the blood flow to some part of the brain is cut off, the brain cells there soon begin to die. If they were cells that controlled body movements, the stroke victim may become paralyzed. Death of other brain cells can result in a loss of the ability to speak.

The main cause of strokes is high blood pressure, which may cause a weak spot in a blood vessel to burst open or may contribute to blockage of a cholesterol-clogged artery in the brain. So the same factors that increase fat people's risk of heart attacks—high blood pressure and cholesterol—also make them more likely to suffer from strokes than thinner people.

Cancer is the number-two killer in the United States today—and in opinion polls it is usually the disease people say they fear most. The obese run a far higher risk of getting cancer than others. Fat women have much higher than usual rates of cancers of the breast, ovaries, uterus, and cervix. For overweight men, there is a higher-than-normal risk of cancers of the colon, rectum, and prostate.

Millions of Americans suffer from diabetes. There are really two different types: insulin-dependent diabetes (Type I), which strikes mostly the young, and non-insulin-dependent diabetes (Type II). The vast majority of diabetics have Type II—

and most of them are overweight. Diabetes can kill. It is also the leading cause of blindness in this country, and the number-one cause for amputations as well. The circulation of diabetics is very bad. Because of this, their eyes do not receive enough blood, and some of the sight cells die. As a result, many diabetics become blind. Their arms and legs may also have a poor blood supply; cells are starved and die, and gangrene often sets in. Gangrene might spread to vital parts of the body like the heart and lungs, and threaten the person's life; only cutting off the limb may save the patient. Here, too, the obese suffer more than others.

Other Health Problems

For a long time we have known that fat people suffer more diseases caused by bacteria and viruses than do those of normal weight. Now we know why. A person's immune system fights disease. In part, the immune system is made up of a whole variety of white blood cells that fight germs either by attacking them directly or by making chemicals that poison those germs. Well, studies have shown that fat people's immune defenses are less active and effective than those of normal-weight people.

Mental illness is another serious health problem. Millions of Americans suffer from such ailments as schizophrenia and depression. In schizophrenia, a person withdraws into a world of his or her own. In depression, a person cannot enjoy simple pleasures. Going to a movie or seeing a ball game seems uninteresting. Even meeting people is a turn-off. Life seems hopeless. Fat people have been found to suffer from both these disorders far more often than people of normal weight.

Many things may contribute to mental illness. Researchers have found evidence that heredity can make certain people more likely to suffer from schizophrenia or depression, and there are some distinctive differences in their brain chemistry. But a person's interactions with the world can also play an important role; negative experiences can produce stress that brings on illness. Fat people encounter plenty of negative experiences in today's world, and in general they don't think very well of themselves. Their poor self-image influences the way they look at life.

The list of health problems for the obese goes on

and on. They have a greater risk of breathing and sleep problems. People who are fat fall down more often, suffering from fractures and other complications. Their weight puts a strain on the knees. After all, with every step, those poor, overworked knees have to carry the weight of the whole body. Arthritis often develops and makes walking very difficult.

The obese suffer more from gout and gallstone problems; they have more appendicitis attacks—in fact, more of just about every ailment you can think of.

When scientists looked closely at fat people, they made a very surprising discovery. The dangers of obesity depend more on where the fat is—how it is distributed among various parts of the body—than on the total amount of fat a person has. There are two basic patterns: the "apple," in which body fat is found mainly around the middle of the body, and the "pear," with fat concentrated in the lower body and thighs. The "apple" pattern is more typical of men, and the "pear" is a typical female pattern, but each type is found in members of both sexes. Both men and women with fat concentrated around the middle of the body—in a thick waist ("spare tire"), a potbelly, or "love handles"—have been found to have more heart disease, strokes, diabetes, and other health problems than equally fat people whose fat is concentrated in their thighs, hips, or buttocks. The difference seems to be associated with the response of the fat tissue to insulin, a hormone that plays key roles in determining the body's use of sugars and fats.

Benefits of Losing Weight

When obese people are able to get rid of some of their extra pounds, the results are very encouraging. In experiments that closely followed obese people who lost weight, a very great improvement was already observed when the patients had lost 10 percent of their original weight. (In other words, a two hundred-pound man would have to lose only twenty pounds to reduce his health risks.) In one study, nearly half of the people with high blood pressure were able to give up their medicine after they had lost just 10 percent of their original weight. Their cholesterol levels improved dramatically, and their triglycerides went down, too. In

another study, one third of the diabetics who lost
10 percent of their weight were able to give up
their medications. Another quarter could cut down
drastically, with no ill effects. In still a third study,
when obese patients with liver problems lost just 10
percent of their weight, in most cases all signs of
liver disorders disappeared. (These patients were
not suffering from any known disease such as liver
cancer or alcoholic cirrhosis.) In all these studies, it
was noticed that the people who benefited the most
were those who lost their fat mainly from their
bellies rather than their thighs or buttocks.

Best of all, nearly all the people who lost those
pounds felt better afterward. When extremely
overweight people think about all the pounds they
need to lose to get down to their ideal weight, they
may feel discouraged. That goal may seem impossible. But if they can feel better and improve their
health with a loss of just 10 percent, that seems like
a much more realistic goal to aim for.

WHERE THE
FOOD GOES

HOW DO PEOPLE get fat? By eating more food than their bodies need. In the next chapter we'll find out what scientists have learned about how and why some people become obese while others—who may actually eat more—do not. But first we need to know more about food—what's in it and what happens to it after it is eaten.

When food is taken into the body, much of it is in the form of rather complicated chemicals. During the processes of digestion, these chemicals are broken down into simpler forms. The body uses some of them for building and repairing tissues and for making other useful body chemicals. Some of the food serves as a source of energy. When the food supplied to the body is more than it needs for energy and building materials, the excess is changed into fats, which are stored away in various parts of the body.

Fats

Just what is fat? If you pinch up a fold of skin from your belly or sides, you hold in your hand a combination of different kinds of tissues. The outer skin is really very thin. Beneath it is connective tissue. This is a very complex combination of cells that help to give the body shape and provide protective cushioning for the organs inside. One type of connective-tissue cell is the *fat cell*, named because it contains fat deposits. When fat cells are full, they are round and plump. When their fat reserves have been used up, they shrink in. But no matter how much weight a person loses, the fat cells never disappear—they are still there, ready to store fat again when there is an excess of food.

A chemist would define a fat as a "triglyceryl ester of a fatty acid." For the average person, it is enough to know that a fat is a kind of chemical the body uses for a number of purposes. One of the most important is as an energy reserve. Fat is a more concentrated energy source than any other food material.

Fats are found in many different foods. Dairy products such as milk, cheeses, and butter contain them. Meats, nuts, and oils are also rich in fats.

Perhaps you have heard about "saturated" and "unsaturated" fats. The distinction refers to the kind of chemical bonds they contain. Unsaturated compounds have one or more "hot spots," bonds that take part very readily in chemical reactions; saturated compounds tend to be more stable. There is some evidence that saturated fats in the diet contribute to the formation of cholesterol deposits in the blood vessels and may lead to heart and circulatory problems. Meats and dairy products contain mainly saturated fats, while unsaturated fats are found in vegetable oils. But unsaturated fats are so reactive that they can combine with oxygen from the air, giving foods a rancid or "spoiled" taste. Manufacturers sometimes treat vegetable oils to be used in food products to make them less reactive and thus keep the foods from spoiling. In such cases the labels may say "hardened" or "partially hydrogenated" vegetable oil, which means that it contains saturated fats.

The average American's diet contains about 40 percent fats. Doctors believe that ought to be cut down to 30 percent or less for good health.

Carbohydrates

Although fats are the richest "energy foods," the main source of energy for the body is actually a different class of food chemicals, the *carbohydrates*. The two main types of carbohydrates are *sugars* and *starches*. Sugars give fruits their sweet taste. Grains such as corn, rice, and wheat and vegetables such as potatoes and beans are plentiful sources of food starch.

Starches are really long chains of simple sugars. If you eat a cracker, for instance, your body will break it down into the sugar, glucose. Digestion starts right in your mouth, as chemicals in saliva work on the starch. (Try chewing a mouthful of plain crackers longer than you normally would, and you will discover that it is beginning to taste sweet.) Glucose is the most common sugar. The body converts it into the energy it needs for moving, thinking, talking—just about everything.

When food supplies more sugar than the body needs, the excess can be stored away in the liver in the form of a starch called glycogen. The body can also convert sugars to fats, which is the reason people can get fat if they eat too much candy and cake, or gorge themselves on starchy foods like breads and pasta.

Proteins

Proteins are a third kind of chemical found in the foods we eat. Proteins are the main building materials of the body, and they are especially important for growth and repair. Special proteins called enzymes act like chemical "traffic police," directing and controlling the thousands of chemical reactions that take place in the body. Still other proteins are hormones, which serve as a chemical signal system that helps to coordinate body activities. All together, scientists think that there may be as many as one hundred thousand kinds of proteins in the body, each one performing a different task.

Proteins are very large and complex chemicals, formed from simpler units called *amino acids* that are linked together into long chains like the beads in a necklace. There are about twenty different kinds of amino acids in proteins. Imagine how many varied patterns you could form if you were stringing a necklace from beads of twenty different colors. When you consider that the chains in proteins are typically hundreds or thousands of amino acids long, the possibilities for variation are almost limitless.

Actually, the proteins in the foods we eat are quite useless—at least in the form in which they occur. When you eat a ham-and-cheese sandwich, for example, you are taking in pig proteins in the ham, cow proteins in the cheese, and wheat proteins in the bread. Each one is somewhat different from human proteins, but they are all formed from the same amino acid building blocks. To be used by your body, all the animal and plant proteins in foods must first be broken down into amino acids. That occurs during digestion, in the stomach and intestines. The individual amino acids are small enough to pass through the walls of the intestines and then into tiny blood vessels. They are carried in the blood to various parts of the body and reassembled into various human proteins.

The human liver is equipped to manufacture a dozen amino acids from sugars and other body chemicals. But our bodies cannot make the other eight amino acids commonly found in proteins. These are known as the essential amino acids. If we don't get enough of them in foods, we can't produce the proteins we need to grow, to repair injuries, and to keep the various chemical reactions going. Without the essential amino acids a person could waste away, even on a diet that seems to provide enough food. That is exactly what happens in some parts of the world where people eat mainly grains and vegetable products whose proteins do not contain enough of the essential amino acids. You may have seen pictures of starving children with big bloated bellies and tiny, wasted limbs. They were suffering from this condition, called kwashiorkor. It kills millions of young children every year.

Although food proteins are used mainly as building materials, the body can also draw on them as an energy source, first breaking them down to amino acids and then converting those to sugars.

When a person is starving and no food is available, the proteins in muscles are gradually broken down and used to generate energy. This can be a problem when a person is trying to lose weight by dieting.

Unlike fats and carbohydrates, which are made up of just three elements (carbon, hydrogen, and oxygen), proteins contain another element in addition: nitrogen. When amino acids are converted to sugars or other biochemicals, nitrogen may be released in the form of ammonia, which is a rather poisonous compound. Normally, only very tiny amounts of ammonia are formed—not enough to do any harm—and the body quickly reuses them in producing new amino acids or converts them to a less poisonous nitrogen compound, urea. This is the main form of nitrogen that is flushed out with other body wastes, in the urine and sweat. Some fad diets, though, contain unusually large amounts of protein, and disposing of all the extra nitrogen wastes may cause problems for the body.

Other Food Substances

In addition to fats, carbohydrates, and proteins, the body needs small amounts of simple chemicals such as iron, copper, calcium, zinc, potassium, and a number of others. These are *minerals*. Many of them form a part of the proteins in our bodies. Others work with another class of chemical known as vitamins.

Vitamins are food chemicals that the body needs and cannot make on its own. They play a number of important roles in the body's reactions, contributing to the work and health of the skin and bones, to the action of nerves that permit us to think and move and feel, to the healing of wounds and the defenses against invading microbes. A number of vitamins have been discovered and identified. First they were named by letters of the alphabet (vitamins A and C, for example, and a whole family of B vitamins), and then, as more was learned about them, they received chemical names as well. Vitamin C, for example, is a chemical called *ascorbic acid*, and vitamin E is *tocopherol*.

The list of needed vitamins varies for each species. If humans do not get a steady supply of vitamin C in their food, for instance, they develop bleeding gums and other unpleasant symptoms of scurvy; but ascorbic acid isn't a vitamin for dogs, cats, rats, or most other animals—they can make their own. (The only other common animal species that shares our need for a food source of vitamin C is the guinea pig.)

Still another important part of a good diet is a substance that isn't really a food, since we cannot digest it. This is *fiber*, which is found in most fruits, vegetables, and whole grains. Early humans got a lot more fiber in their diet than we do because they ate more leafy vegetables, fruits, nuts, and whole grains. (The natural fiber is removed from the processed flour used in modern bread, cake, and pasta.) The low-fiber diet that most modern people eat results in constipation and other digestive problems. Today supplements of oat bran and other forms of dietary fiber are becoming popular, mainly because of research suggesting that a fiber-rich diet can reduce the chances of getting cancer and heart disease.

Water is another necessary part of the diet that is not really a nutrient. About two thirds of the weight of your body is water. Each day you lose water in urine, feces, sweat, tears, and even the air you exhale. This water must be replaced—a person could survive for weeks without eating, but no one can live for more than a few days without water. We obtain part of the water we need by drinking beverages, but most of the foods we eat are (like our own bodies) about two thirds water. Some water is also produced in chemical reactions that take place in the body.

But what does eating a balanced diet, one that contains enough proteins, carbohydrates, and fats, as well as vitamins, minerals, and other things, have to do with obesity? To understand the connection, we need to know more about how the body uses food.

Energy and Metabolism

The body uses food for many different purposes, such as growth, repair, and maintaining normal body functions. But everything in the body would stop—immediately—without energy to power the thousands of chemical reactions going on inside us.

This energy comes from the fats, carbohydrates, and proteins in our diet. Food energy is measured in the form of *Calories.* A single Calorie provides enough energy to raise the temperature of a kilogram of water one degree centigrade. Put another way, it will warm up a quart of milk nearly two degrees Fahrenheit.

You have probably seen the energy unit written as "calorie." Strictly speaking, that is an error—and a rather large one, too. A calorie, with a small *c*, is the amount of energy needed to raise one *gram* of water one degree centigrade. The "calories" in foods that people talk about are actually kilocalories (kilo means 1,000), or "large calories," properly shortened to Calories. So a glass of milk contains about 150 Calories, or *150,000* calories! Over the years, though, it has become the custom to use "calorie"—with a small c—for "large calorie" in discussions of nutrition. We will use that convention through the rest of this book.

We need energy for just about everything we do: walking, running, singing, even thinking. Our bodies are always warm, even in the coldest weather. That requires energy. If a person were to stay in bed all day and not get up to drink or eat, he or she would still need a certain amount of energy to breathe and keep the body cells alive and working. The sum of all the chemical reactions that take place in the body is called *metabolism*. Practically all of these reactions use energy.

The minimum amount of energy needed to keep just the necessary parts of us going is called the *basal metabolic rate* or BMR. Everyone has his or her own BMR. To some degree it depends upon how much you weigh, and how fast your body normally burns its fuel. A child's metabolic rate is nearly twice that of an adult, but the BMR drops rapidly through the growing years and then declines more slowly after age eighteen or so. For the average young woman the BMR is about 1,400 calories, and for the average young man it is 1,700 calories. But few of us stay in bed all day, so we use more calories each day than our BMR. A student or an office worker, who spends much of the day sitting and does not get much exercise, might use up about 2,500 calories a day. A lumberjack, who spends the day at hard physical labor outdoors in cold weather, requires more than 8,000 calories a day to supply all his body needs. In middle and old age, the continuing decline of the BMR may produce a tendency to gain weight if people still continue to eat the same amounts of food.

If you eat exactly enough food to satisfy your body's daily needs, your weight will stay constant. If you eat more calories than you need, your body will store the excess as fat, and your weight will rise. If you eat fewer calories than you need each day, you will lose weight.

It seems like such a simple set of equations: If you want to lose weight, just eat fewer calories or burn more energy each day (or some combination of the two approaches). Putting those ideas into practice, though, turns out to be far more complicated.

Calories do count, but all foods are not alike in their calorie contents. For instance, carbohydrates, when burned in the body, will give about four calories for each gram that is consumed. (A gram of sugar or starch is about the size of the eraser at the end of a pencil.) Proteins also give about four calories per gram when they are converted to energy. But fats pack a much larger energy wallop. Each gram of fat contains about nine calories.

Think about that difference for a moment, and you will realize it has two important implications for losing weight. First, a good way to lose weight is to cut down on fats in the diet and emphasize the lower-energy carbohydrates and proteins instead. People who want to lose weight should stay away from fatty meats, chocolate candies, butter, ice cream, and other fatty foods.

The second implication is a bit less encouraging. The weight dieters are trying to lose is body *fat*, not protein or carbohydrate. But fat is the most concentrated energy source of all. To burn off a single pound of fat, you must use up 3,500 calories. Weight-loss plans that promise to help you lose a pound a day or more are just hype. Unless you are a lumberjack, you probably could not use up 3,500 calories a day, even if you ate practically nothing. (And if you tried eating practically nothing for a few days in a row, you would soon be too weak to do much more than lie in bed all day—which would use up only 1,400 to 1,700 calories.)

Losing a pound a *week*, though, is a more realistic goal. If you normally burn 2,500 calories a day, let us say, doing what you normally do, then if you cut the food you eat down to only 2,000 calories, your body will be 500 calories short. It will have to use 500 calories of stored energy. Keeping your food intake the same but increasing your activity to burn up an extra 500 calories each day would have the same effect. And 500 calories a day for seven days totals 3,500 calories—a pound of fat lost.

6

WHY DO PEOPLE GET FAT?

WHY ARE SOME people overweight while others stay thin? Many people would say the answer is easy: Fat people eat too much.

But how much is "too much"? Many fat people claim they don't really eat very much—no more than people of normal weight. Are they lying? Or perhaps mistaken? After all, it's easy to forget a little between-meals snack here or there, and people often eat without really paying attention to what they are doing. (Do you count how many kernels of popcorn you munch while you are watching a movie?) Most people are not very accurate in estimating the sizes of food portions; they also may not realize which foods are more fattening than others.

(Who would think that innocent-looking pat of butter on the baked potato contains more calories than the whole potato!)

Researchers who have studied people's eating habits, observing and measuring what is actually eaten under carefully controlled conditions, have made some surprising discoveries. It's true that fat people do tend to eat somewhat more than they report they did—but so do people of normal weight. What's more, both overweight people and normal-weight people underestimate their food consumption by about the same amount. And though some overweight people do gorge themselves, there are others who really do eat only normal amounts of food and yet still manage to gain weight.

Apparently the explanations for overweight are not so simple, after all, and there is no one explanation to fit everybody.

Environment

Cultural traditions have much to do with how heavy the average person is. In Japan, for instance, very few people are overweight. And yet, when Japanese families move to the United States, as the influence of traditional customs declines, their weight, on the average, goes up. After a few generations, they are just as fat as Americans of other ancestry.

We have already seen that even within a culture, fashions can change dramatically. The ideal figure today is much slimmer than it was a few centuries—or even a few generations—ago. Our society is prejudiced against overweight people, and children grow up with the attitude that thin is beautiful. Yet medical statistics show that, on the average, Americans are getting heavier—even the children. So cultural influences cannot be the whole story.

Another aspect of our modern civilization may be having a far greater effect on our weight. We are much less physically active than people of past generations. Perhaps your grandparents have told about how they used to walk miles to school each day. Now most children go by bus or other means of transportation. Most of the school hours are spent sitting in classrooms, and the after-school hours that used to be filled with chores around the farm or ball games on the city streets are now most likely spent sitting in front of a TV set. It is not surprising that today's children are not only heavier but less fit than children in the past. A study of six- to seventeen-year-olds, reported in 1989 by the Amateur Athletic Union, showed that only 32 percent of American children had satisfactory scores in tests of strength, flexibility, and endurance—compared with 43 percent ten years ago.

The foods we eat today also contribute to overweight. The foods the government donates to school lunch programs are mainly high-fat items such as ground beef, pork, and luncheon meats. As a result, many nutritionists believe, school lunches often have too high a proportion of fat. The meals at home are often no better. Many families rely heavily on fast foods, which typically contain between 40 and 55 percent fat. (Six chicken nuggets, for example, have 310 calories, including about 180 calories of fat.)

Today's adults, too, have a much more sedentary way of life. Far more people work at desk jobs or other occupations that require little physical effort than was the case a generation or two ago. At home, modern appliances have removed much of the drudgery—and the exercise—from household chores. We pop a load of dirty clothes into an automatic washer, for example, flick a few dials, and then come back half an hour later to transfer the laundry to the dryer; people used to spend hours of heavy labor scrubbing the clothes on a washboard, wringing them out, and hanging them up to dry. Modern Americans use much of the time they save on household chores for watching television—a recent study reported that the typical American family watches forty-nine hours of TV a week!

TV watching can contribute to obesity in two ways. First, it is a passive activity, which does not use up many calories over the BMR. Second, it often leads to extra eating. The many commercials for food products set the watchers' digestive juices flowing. They begin to think about food and start feeling hungry; soon enough, they make a trip to the refrigerator for a snack. TV watchers often munch away at food absentmindedly, without any conscious thought. It becomes a habit—something to do.

Actually, one of the things in our modern environment that contributes to obesity—and makes it very difficult to lose weight—is that food is all too readily available. "The American refrigerator is bulging with food," says Dr. Theodore Van Itallie, a researcher on obesity. "It's the American habit to eat from the refrigerator at all times of the day."

Most of us learn our eating habits in our early years. Many parents urge their children to eat up everything on their plates and sometimes punish them if they refuse. Trying to please their parents, children learn to eat even when they are already full. "Finish your peas first, and then you can have some nice dessert," the parent says, and the child learns another unfortunate lesson: Sweet foods— fattening foods—are desirable rewards. The lesson is reinforced, again and again, by many pleasant experiences. Parties and special treats are filled with cakes, candies, ice cream, and other sweet-tasting but calorie-rich things to eat. A piece of candy may be offered as a reward for getting a good grade on a test or doing something else that pleases a parent. Some of our best memories are associated with food.

These pleasant associations lead some people to turn to food as a comfort when they are feeling unhappy. Eating becomes a way to escape from life's problems, a way to cope with stress. Whenever a situation comes up to make them anxious or "nervous," these food-focused people eat. It's a way for them to live with loneliness, or frustration, or anything that might require extra effort. When food binging leads to obesity, the fatness may be used as an excuse. "Nobody really knows me or appreciates me," the person thinks. "There's no point in making an effort." So the obesity becomes a barrier and a cop-out as the person withdraws from attempting to make new friends or face new situations. "It's not my fault," the person thinks. "I've tried to lose weight, but I can't."

A culture that makes it all too easy to gain weight and a variety of psychological factors may contribute to obesity, but this is not the whole story. Obesity is a very complex condition, and physical factors can also contribute to it. They involve the body and the way it handles food.

Body Differences

As we have seen in the previous chapter, we "burn" some of the digested food to obtain the energy that our body cells need to survive. But each of us has a different BMR. That is, each of us burns food differently. Some people's bodies are more efficient than others; they have a low BMR and can get enough energy for the body's needs out of a small amount of food. The rest of the calories they eat are stored away in fat deposits. Efficiency is normally a good thing, and it is here, too, for people who are continually faced with the threat of starvation. But that is not the case for most people in the United States and other developed nations today. When food is plentiful, people with a low BMR become obese, while those with less efficient bodies (a higher BMR) waste a great many calories—and stay thin.

Thermogenesis, the body's production of heat from its food intake, is being studied by hundreds of scientists all over the world. Some of their findings are causing doctors to change their ways of dealing with obesity. For years obese people have been accused of being gluttons. If only they could control their appetite and eat less, it was thought, then their problem would be solved. It's true that eating less would help, but many of the obese would have to eat far less than the charts say they should.

Calorie charts are based on what the average person ought to eat to maintain his or her weight. Many obese people, however, should be following a chart that is made for humans with an unusually efficient body-burning engine. So their numbers should be *lower.* "It means that some people have to eat less than others to maintain their weight. It's like what obese people always said, but nobody ever believed," says Dr. Clifton Bogardus of the National Institutes of Health (NIH).

What makes it so difficult for the obese is that they suffer the same hunger pangs as the "normal" population. If they cut down on their food, they are going to become hungry more often. Then it requires a very powerful willpower to say "no" to those tempting bits of food. It's hard for a person to go hungry for much of the day, when TV commercials, magazine ads, billboards, and store window displays continually present mouth-watering displays of food. It is almost impossible to resist the urge to eat when you keep hearing, seeing, and smelling reminders of food throughout the day.

Differences in BMR are not the whole story. Two people might have the same BMR and be similar in age, sex, general body build, and various other ways; yet one might gain far more weight than the other on the same diet. A recent study with Pima Indians has finally given us an answer to this puzzle. When cameras and radar were used to follow these Indians for several days, it was discovered that some of them fidget far more than others. In other words, they may squirm in their chairs, swing a foot back and forth, snap their fingers, or engage in other forms of what scientists call "spontaneous physical activity." Others are far quieter, hardly moving at all. When the scientists who were observing them calculated how many extra calories the fidgeters were using up each day, they were astounded—in some cases the difference was as much as to 800 calories a day, the equivalent of walking briskly for two and a half hours! That means that just from fidgeting, some people can lose an *extra* pound and a half a week!

Other doctors have found important differences in the nervous systems of obese and normal-weight people. For instance, it has long been known that very obese people are more lethargic than thinner people, moving less and reacting more slowly to things. Obese people breathe more slowly, their hearts beat more slowly, and their muscle response is not as quick. They have less adrenaline—the emergency hormone—in their blood.

Heredity

There is a great deal of evidence that these and other differences in body physiology, which determine whether a person is likely to become obese, are hereditary. It has been found, for example, that a few days after they were born, babies of mothers with a low BMR also had a slow-burning metabolism. Within a year, many of these babies were already obese. When doctors looked at women with a high BMR, they found that few of these women's babies had a low BMR, and few became obese.

Such differences can help to explain the common observation that obesity tends to run in families. Studies have shown, for instance, that a child born to parents of normal weight has a 7 percent chance of becoming overweight. But if either parent is obese, then in about half the cases their child will be obese. If both parents are grossly overweight, there is an 80 percent chance their child will be overweight, too.

Among Pima Indians, being overweight is a very common problem. Nearly 50 percent of the adults over thirty-five years of age are obese, compared to about 25 percent of the American population in that age group.

Such observations by themselves do not really prove that overweight is hereditary. Perhaps overweight parents just tend to overfeed their children. Studies of adopted children, however, show that this is not the explanation. Records of over five hundred adopted children in Norway, for example, revealed that the adopted children most closely resembled their biological parents. In other words, if the mother who gave birth to the child was obese, and the child was adopted and raised by parents of normal weight, that child was very likely to be obese.

In another study, adopted children were found to resemble their adoptive parents in weight—but only as long as they lived with them. Once the children moved away and lived on their own, their weights changed to more closely resemble those of their biological parents.

Studies of identical twins have also yielded striking results. Such twins come from the same egg and thus have identical genes. The studies show that if one twin is obese at the age of twenty, chances are twice as high that the other twin will also be obese, compared to normal-weight twins. These results were observed whether the twins were raised together or were adopted and raised separately.

Studies like these are leading more and more specialists to believe that most overweight people are born to be fat—it's in their genes. "Obese people are born with a handicap," says Dr. Jules Hirsch, a researcher at Rockefeller University who is highly respected in the field of obesity problems.

Research is gradually casting more light on the nature of this inborn handicap and suggesting ways it may be overcome. Keys to the answers seem to lie in the hormones and other body messengers that stimulate eating and control the handling of food in the body.

Appetite and Obesity

Moving with the crowd at a party, you find yourself at a table holding a bowl full of salted cashew nuts. Will you eat them? If so, will you just take one or two nuts, or will you dip into the bowl again and again until it is nearly empty?

Many things will influence your actions. Some are psychological. If you don't particularly like cashew nuts, you may not be tempted by them at all. But if you are finding the party a disappointment, with no one really interesting to talk to, you may nibble on a few nuts simply for something to do. If you have been worrying about your weight, you may make a conscious effort not to eat the nuts, even if they are one of your favorite foods. How recently, and how much, you have eaten will also influence your desire to sample the nuts—but the amount of the influence, surprisingly, may depend on whether you are overweight or not. Studies have shown that normal-weight people are usually prompted to eat by hunger and don't eat excessive amounts even of particularly tasty foods. Obese people, by contrast, are much more influenced by taste and tend to overeat their favorite foods even when they are not hungry.

Appetite—the urge to eat—is thus rather complicated. Its main function is to prompt people to eat when hunger pangs signal that the body's food reserves need restocking, but it is also influenced by signals from the brain. Appetite may be stimulated when a person is still full from a recent meal. (Have you noticed how you may feel absolutely stuffed after the main course, yet still can "find a little room for dessert"?) An unpleasant experience or an illness can "turn off" appetite even when the body is hungry. Lack of appetite can become a life-threatening complication in some serious diseases, such as cancer and AIDS, and artificial feeding may be necessary to provide the patient with nourishment.

A part of the brain called the *hypothalamus* contains a number of control centers that send messages to various parts of the body to regulate important body processes. Hypothalamic centers even control strong emotions such as anger, fear, and pleasure. So researchers were not surprised to discover that the control center for appetite is also found in the hypothalamus. Actually, two different centers play major roles in appetite. One, the *hunger center*, sends signals telling us we had better eat. The other, the *satiety center*, signals that we've had enough to eat, and so we feel "full."

The appetite centers appear to work differently in the obese and in normal-weight people. For instance, in most normal-weight people, the satiety center responds to exercise by sending out signals of "fullness." For many obese people, however, there is no such response. Even after strenuous exercise, many fat people can sit down to a hearty meal and enjoy every mouthful.

The control centers in the hypothalamus continuously monitor the blood flowing through the brain and respond to changes in the levels of key chemicals. The blood sugar level is one indicator of how well supplied the body's food reserves are. But many important messages are carried in the bloodstream by the specialized chemical messengers called hormones. Researchers have been searching for a hormone that might act as a signal for the appetite centers. Hungarian scientist Joseph Kroll has discovered a hormone, which he named *satietin*, that acts on the satiety center in the hypothalamus. Injections of the hormone cause animals to feel full and refuse food, even if they have not eaten for some time. Since satietin is a natural substance, Dr. Kroll found none of the harmful side effects that accompany some of the appetite suppressants dieting people take to lose weight.

Richard Wurtman at MIT and other researchers

feel that *serotonin*, a chemical that affects the action of some important brain cells, plays an important role in appetite. Interestingly, serotonin also helps to control our mood—whether we are sad or happy—as well. It has other important jobs, too. But understanding its role in appetite might yield better ways to control the weight problem of the obese.

Many overweight people have a craving for carbohydrates in the afternoon and again in the evening. Dr. Wurtman found that this happens because the amount of serotonin in the brain is low at these times. The hunger center responds by sending out the signal "I'm hungry!" Eating cookies, candy, and other carbohydrates satisfies the control center. Crackers, pasta, or rice would do, as well. These snacks cause the body to produce the hormone *insulin*. This vital hormone is secreted by the pancreas when the sugar level in the blood rises. Insulin prompts the liver to take up glucose (sugar) molecules and store them away in the form of the starch, glycogen; the hormone also causes sugar to enter cells where it is "burned" for energy. High levels of insulin stimulate the appetite and prompt the liver to produce fat, which is transported to the body's fat deposits; in young children, insulin stimulates the formation of new fat cells.

Meanwhile, insulin also paves the way for the amino acid *tryptophan* to pass into the brain. There it is changed into serotonin. Soon messages are sent to various parts of the brain. Then the "all is well" signal comes back as the mood centers and appetite centers are satisfied with soothing stimuli.

Dr. Wurtman and other scientists feel that tryptophan would make a safe and effective weight-control chemical. Patients taking this amino acid regularly in the form of a pill two or three times a day have reported that their appetites are under better control, and many have lost pounds this way. Millions of people had taken this over-the-counter diet supplement, either for weight loss or as a sleep aid (its product, serotonin, also helps to "turn on" the brain's sleep center) when troubling reports began to appear in 1989. Hundreds of people who had taken tryptophan pills suddenly developed an ordinarily rare blood disorder, and some of them died. Researchers suspected the culprit might be some impurity in the pills, rather than tryptophan itself, but the products were taken off the market while medical scientists searched for the answer.

James Gibbs, a psychiatrist at Cornell University Medical School, says that "behavior as complex as feeding and satiety is probably determined by multiple controlling factors." He believes one of these, in addition to insulin and satietin, is *cholecystokinin*, or CCK.

It has long been known that when we eat a meal, CCK is secreted by cells lining the intestines. CCK passes into the blood and signals the satiety center that we have just eaten a meal. The larger the meal, the more CCK is produced; at a certain level, we feel "full."

An interesting finding is that certain cells in the brain also manufacture this hormone.

When patients suffering from bulimia nervosa have been given CCK, many of them stopped binging on food. They lost their appetite.

Adipsin is still another hormone that has been found to play a role in appetite in studies of rats, mice, and other animals. Adipsin is produced by fat cells. Like CCK, it gives signals to the satiety center in the hypothalamus. Obese mice and rats were found to have abnormally low levels of this hormone. If this is also found to be true in humans, it could have great importance in our battle against obesity.

Natural painkillers produced in the brain, called *beta endorphins*, have been found to stimulate appetite. Like narcotic drugs such as morphine, endorphins produce feelings of euphoria, and they have been linked with the addictive effects of a number of compulsive behaviors. Long-distance running, for example, has been found to stimulate endorphin production and produces a euphoric "runner's high." This good feeling that comes after a long run is what makes runners continue their habit day after day, in cold or hot weather, in spite of rain or snow.

Many obese individuals appear to have an unusually high level of endorphins. Naloxone, a drug that counteracts the effects of endorphins, has been found to greatly reduce the appetite. Naltrexone, a closely related and safer chemical, is now being tried by researchers as a way to control obesity.

Estrogens, the female sex hormones, stimulate the appetite. Many women have increased appetites as they near their menstrual periods, when their estrogen level is especially high. In one study at the University of Toronto, researchers found that women ate 20 to 25 percent more food just before menstruation than they did early in their period. One twenty-eight-year-old patient admitted, "Just before my period I eat a lot of sweet things like chocolate and cookies."

Fat Cells

For years doctors felt that a fat infant was doomed to be a fat adult. They believed that most of a person's fat cells are formed in the first two years of life. Hence, a baby who is overfed at that time will produce an excess of fat cells. But recent research casts serious doubt on that belief. As Dr. Leona Shapiro, nutritionist at the University of California (Berkeley), has said, "Just because you have a fat baby doesn't mean you should become alarmed and immediately try to thin that child down."

A newborn baby comes equipped with five or six billion fat cells. During the first two years, many more are indeed formed. During puberty, though, there is a spurt of new fat-cell formation. (The resulting changes in body contours may prompt teenagers to regard themselves—perhaps incorrectly—as "fat.") By the time the average person becomes an adult, he or she may have as many as 30 or 40 billion fat cells. An obese adult, on the other hand, may have as many as 80 to 120 billion.

It is not just the number of fat cells that causes overweight problems. Their size is equally important. These cells can vary from shriveled, almost empty structures to heavy, bulging masses, filled with fats. Just about all the fats in the body are stored in these special fat cells that scientists call *adipose cells.*

One unfortunate thing about fat cells is that they seem to have an urge to become full. So after a person has dieted with great pain and effort, hunger pangs become an everyday torture. The undersize cells apparently send out signals to the appetite center, almost demanding a meal to fill them.

Is it any wonder that the vast majority of severely obese people who have lost a lot of weight eventually regain every pound they lost? At the bottom of it all are those fat cells. As we saw in Chapter 5, no matter how severe the diet, not a single fat cell is lost, and each is demanding more fat.

The fat in fat cells is made up of fatty acids and glycerol. These substances are continually broken down and remade again. When a person is well fed, and the fat cells are satisfied, there is an abundance of fatty acids and glycerol in the blood and this sends a signal to the appetite center that all is well, and eating is unnecessary. But when one is dieting, the fatty acid and glycerol levels drop drastically, and one feels hungry. During severe diets, the thyroid gland slows down its production of hormones that direct the burning of food for energy, the white blood cell activity drops, the blood pressure is subnormal, the pulse rate slows, and people feel colder than normal.

Some recent experiments, which will be discussed in Chapter 8, suggest that an enzyme called *lipoprotein lipase (LPL)* may also play a key role in weight gain and dieting. This enzyme promotes the storage of fat in the body's fat cells. Dieting promotes an increase in LPL levels and thus makes it easier for the shrunken fat cells to plump up again.

When scientists have examined the fat cells very closely, they have discovered two special proteins on their surface. They have been named $alpha_2$ receptors and $beta_1$ receptors. The $alpha_2$ receptors cause fat cells to store extra fat, while the $beta_1$ do just the opposite: The fat cells lose their fat, and the person becomes thinner.

Men seem to have more alpha$_2$ receptors in the region of the abdomen. That's why so many middle-aged men develop potbellies—the typical male "apple" pattern of fat distribution. Women seem to have more in their hips and buttocks. That's where they tend to get fat, in the typical female "pear" shape. When a man diets, he finds it very hard to lose weight in his belly, and women find it difficult to lose weight in the hips and buttocks. The pounds may fall away easily in other areas, though.

Other studies have found another key difference in fat distribution. The fat tissue from the upper body contains a moderate number of rather large cells, while that from the lower body contains a larger number of smaller fat cells.

Although people appear to be stuck with their fat cells for life, scientists may be able to offer some hope of reducing them, someday. In studies on sheep and other animals, they have made antibodies that attach to fat cells. The body then destroys these fat cells. They are gone forever! Will this work with humans? Probably. Is it safe? Time will tell.

The Set Point Theory

Many food scientists believe that both obesity and the difficulties of losing weight are explained by the set point theory. This theory states that the body tends to maintain its original weight. If a person binges and gains an excess number of pounds, after a time he or she will return to the original weight—the "set point." On the other hand, if a person goes on a strict diet, losing many pounds, he or she becomes irritable, depressed, and lethargic as long as the weight remains at the lower level. The metabolic rate drops and the person thinks about food all the time.

Is there any hope, then, for the obese, if this theory is correct? Yes, for by exercising regularly one can change the set point. This will permit a loss of pounds while still maintaining normal body reactions and feelings.

ADDICTED
TO FOOD?

WE ALL HAVE to eat. If we didn't, our bodies wouldn't get the nutrients we need to continue functioning, and we would die. Most people enjoy eating. It's one of life's simple pleasures that we often look forward to. But for some people food becomes the center of attention. They can't stop thinking about food. It becomes an obsession and a compulsion, and some would say an addiction.

There are several ways a person can be said to be addicted to food. All of them involve a constant focus on eating. The most obvious "food addict" is a person who compulsively overeats. But others, who suffer from anorexia nervosa, are equally obsessed with food but force themselves *not* to eat.

Bulimia nervosa can be regarded as still another food addiction, in which a person goes on food binges, eating uncontrollably, then purging out the food.

It's easy to see how food can gain such importance in a person's life that it can become a psychological addiction. It is a basic need that is one of the first to be filled when we are young. A baby cries when it is hungry, and food calms the child as well as the parents' nerves. In the years that follow, as we saw in the last chapter, sweets and treats are often rewards for good behavior. They may be a consolation, too, when things don't go well. When we are older, meals become an important time for social interaction—with families at dinnertime, or friends in the school cafeteria; food can be an important thing we share together. Even adults recognize the importance of eating in our lives. Some of the most important business deals and decisions are made over lunch. And what is more romantic than a candlelit dinner?

Traditionally, eating disorders were thought to be due to psychological problems. But research is providing insights that point to biochemical causes. This would suggest that the problem is much more than a psychological one; it could be a physical addiction problem.

The Biochemistry of Food Addiction

A good meal is usually a pleasurable experience. Some brain researchers believe that the pleasant feelings a hot fudge sundae brings are actually a natural high produced by chemicals in the brain. They believe that certain foods, as well as other pleasures in life (like watching a good movie, listening to music we enjoy, or exercising), stimulate the production of natural morphinelike painkillers, the endorphins, which are produced by the body to help relieve discomfort and stress.

Research by psychologist Elliott Blass at Johns Hopkins University has suggested that sweets may stimulate endorphin production. In an experiment with rats he found that sugar has a morphinelike calming effect. Naltrexone, a drug that blocks the production of endorphins, seems to block the calming effects of sugar as well.

The appetite-stimulating effects of endorphins were mentioned in the last chapter. These chemicals are produced in times of stress, or when we have not eaten in a while. They help to restore the body's energy reserves, by making us desire protein and fats. Indeed, in laboratory tests, rats that were injected with morphine ate more protein and fat, but when injected with a drug that blocks morphine, they did not have this craving.

Some experts believe that in eating disorders something goes wrong with the natural balance of endorphin production, and the person becomes addicted to the endorphins produced. Applying this theory to bulimics, eating binges may be the result of a chemical imbalance. But each eating binge then further contributes to the imbalance. Research at the University of Wisconsin in Madison indicates that bulimic patients do indeed have higher levels of endorphins in their blood than normal people. Jeffrey Jonas, at Fair Oaks Hospital in Summit, New Jersey, has reported success in treating bulimic patients with drugs that block endorphin production.

Other researchers are studying anorexia nervosa. Mary Ann Marrazzi and Elliot Luby at Wayne State University in Detroit believe that psychological factors cause young women to be concerned about their weight and to begin severe and strict diets. Then, after about three months, their bodies actually become addicted to dieting. The addiction becomes so strong that patients will continue dieting even when they know they are seriously ill.

Many in the medical field disagree with the endorphin theory. They argue that if it were true, then anyone who dieted for a long time could become anorexic, but this just isn't the case, and the condition, although growing, is still found mainly in young women.

The Wayne State researchers answer this objection with the theory that anorexics have an inherited weakness in the system of natural brain opiates. Our bodies are designed so that the opiates (endorphins) are produced to protect against starvation by helping the body to conserve energy and resources. Endorphin production causes a coupled response. This means that it prompts two different body responses, and that one occurs when the other one does. Endorphins cause the body's metabolic activity to fall to the bare minimum needed to survive. (Many anorexics find their heartbeat slows down, and in most cases so much weight is lost that they no longer have their monthly menstrual cycle.

When faced with starvation, the body will stop all unnecessary functions that are not directly needed to survive.) At the same time, endorphins are designed to stimulate the craving for food, so that the person will eat more and not starve. In anorexia-prone people, something goes wrong and the responses become uncoupled. The body becomes addicted to endorphins, and the craving for food disappears.

In testing this theory the researchers treated eight anorexic patients who were hospitalized for their condition with the opiate-blocking drug naltrexone. They theorized that the drug would block the effects of the body's endorphins so that the anorexics would not get their usual high from dieting. The results seemed to support the theory: Six of the anorexic patients gained weight while on the drug; one was back to her normal weight and began menstruating again.

Critics of the study say that the results were meaningless. Nine out of ten anorexic patients in a good hospital program will gain weight while in the program. Although many recover from anorexia, there is no known "quick cure."

The very nature of an anorexic patient makes it

difficult to determine whether this drug or other treatments are effective. It is extremely hard to get anorexics to continue treatment once they leave the hospital. Once they start gaining weight, they may become frightened and go back to dieting. Like other addicts, they can recover but are never cured of their addiction. They have to avoid dieting for the rest of their lives.

Further support for the idea that anorexia is an addiction is furnished by observations that one fourth to one half of all anorexics are also addicted to substances like alcohol, cocaine, or other drugs. This cross-addiction is a typical addictive pattern.

Wayne State researcher Mary Ann Marrazzi discovered that rats and mice react differently to an injection of morphine. The mouse becomes hyperactive and anorexic, while the rat becomes hungry and tired. "Normal" people react like the rat when they receive morphine, or when their bodies produce natural endorphins. It is a pleasurable experience, but it does not permanently alter their normal eating patterns. But the mouse's reaction is similar to that of an anorexia-prone human.

Researchers are also examining obesity and compulsive overeating in terms of physical and biochemical causes. Evidence suggests that obese people have lower levels of endorphins in their blood. Obese people may be overeating to produce a feeling of well-being, and a cycle develops in which they become addicted to overeating in order to compensate for the lower endorphin levels. In experiments at the Eating Disorders Clinic at the University of Michigan, ten normal-weight women were given a nonaddictive opiatelike drug, butorphanol. When they were offered various snack foods, these women preferred sweet-tasting foods and those high in fats. But when they were given the opiate blocker naloxone along with the synthetic opiate, they tended to turn down chocolate bars and cookies in favor of snacks with fewer fat calories.

It would appear that pleasure and food intake are very closely related. When we're hungry, almost anything smells delicious. Even water tastes "good" when we're thirsty. If the endorphin theories are correct, this is a major advance in our understanding of how people experience pleasure, and why some become addicted to these experiences.

Other researchers are exploring the role of other brain chemicals in appetite and eating patterns.

Sarah Leibowitz, a neurobiologist at New York's Rockefeller University, believes that at different times we experience hunger or craving for different food types. For example, sometimes we're in the mood for a pizza, and other times a thick juicy steak is what we crave. Endorphins and other neurotransmitters control our desire for carbohydrates, fats, and proteins—the three main food groups. But at the same time, the types of food we eat can affect the production of these neurochemicals.

When we drastically change our eating habits, as when we go on a severe diet, the brain chemistry is altered. Sarah Leibowitz observed that experimental rats tend to overeat later, to compensate, when one of their feedings is skipped. She and other researchers believe that dieting techniques like skipping meals or cutting out one of the food types (carbohydrates or fats) can cause confusing signals that change the balance of brain chemicals.

Each of the brain chemicals seems to affect certain specific food types. Dopamine, for example, has the opposite effect to endorphins—it suppresses the desire for protein. Norepinephrine and neuropeptide Y stimulate the desire for carbohydrates. In one Rockefeller University experiment, a rat injected with neuropeptide Y ate as much in four hours as it would normally consume in two days. Rats injected with the neuropeptide and then allowed to choose among carbohydrate, fat, or protein meals always chose the carbohydrates.

Neuropeptide Y normally builds up when rats are without food for a while—for example, before the first meal of the day. This seems to be a means of regulating blood sugar levels through hunger for carbohydrates. But if the rats receive continual injections of neuropeptide Y, chronic overeating and obesity result. Researchers believe that in humans, cycles of surging neurochemicals may set up an addictive condition causing overeating, which may lead to obesity. In the case of bulimics, binge eating and purging may produce surges of the peptide in the brain, or an imbalance could trigger abnormal eating patterns.

Other brain chemicals also seem to play a role in appetite. The neurotransmitter serotonin is one of them, as we saw in the last chapter. It inhibits the desire for carbohydrates. MIT neurochemist Richard Wurtman believes that when we eat carbohydrates more serotonin is produced, so that the next time we eat, we won't eat as many carbohydrates. Maybe this explains why you might not feel in the mood for pizza for lunch if you had a big spaghetti dinner the night before.

Low levels of serotonin and norepinephrine in the brain have been linked to severe depression. Some antidepressant drugs seem to work by increasing serotonin levels in the body. Richard and Judith Wurtman and Harris R. Lieberman at MIT suggest that some obese people may eat carbohydrates to keep from getting depressed. They found that people who typically overeat mostly carbohydrates feel less depressed than those who overeat other types of snacks. These "carbohydrate cravers" could account for up to half of all obese people. Carbohydrate cravers may thus be unconsciously trying to self-medicate for low serotonin levels with high-carbohydrate foods. These foods raise the serotonin levels and improve the eaters' spirits. As carbohydrate snacking is continually used as a way of feeling better, an addictive eating pattern may develop.

Researchers have found that antidepressant drugs such as fluoxetine, which raise serotonin levels, also reduce the tendency to overeat under stress.

The drugs not only relieve depression but decrease carbohydrate snacking as well, and the patients lose weight. Patients who responded to fluoxetine said they ate less because after a few bites they no longer had the urge to eat. Fluoxetine has also shown promising results in treating bulimia.

Food Addiction?

Are eating disorders true addictions? Physical or psychological addictions? Or are they emotional and psychological ways of coping with stress and depression? Are they the result of biochemical processes and imbalances? The specialists do not fully agree about the causes.

At a New York Academy of Sciences conference, experts pointed out that obesity and other food disorders should not be viewed as single disorders with single causes. There are many theories, and some are more useful than others in helping to treat people with food disorders, as we will see later chapters. It does seem evident, however, that the trend in the future will be to focus on the biochemical aspects as we gain a greater understanding of how the body and its inner processes work. Thus future treatments for eating disorders will undoubtedly involve various drug treatments to counter chemical imbalances and break addictive cycles. These breakthroughs will bring better results in the fight against food addictions.

DIET
MANIA

THE ANCIENT GREEK physician Hippocrates prescribed lower-calorie diets for overweight people. More than two thousand years have passed since then, and people are still trying to lose weight by dieting.

Health experts are quite concerned about the millions of dieters. Some experts estimate that the number of overweight Americans is as high as one hundred million (one out of two adults!), but others insist the numbers are *much* lower. They believe that many dieters are at their normal weight before they begin dieting. But this isn't the experts' only concern—dieting can be dangerous!

First of all, if a person does not get the proper

nutrients to keep his or her body functioning properly, health problems can occur. Any diet that consists of less than 1,200 to 1,500 calories a day probably will not provide the body with enough of the nutrients it needs and could be harmful. Recent studies also indicate that people who lose weight rapidly by reduced-calorie diets have a much higher than normal risk of developing gallstones. Health experts, therefore, urge that any low-calorie diet should be conducted only under the supervision of a doctor.

Dieting can be especially dangerous for children. Their growing bodies need more nutrients than those of adults. Except in rare cases, doctors do not recommend that children diet.

Gimmicks and Fads

Dieting, or eating less than normal, is hard to do. So it's not surprising that people eagerly turn to other ways of losing weight. There are thousands of gimmicks and gadgets that promise to get rid of fat forever—usually with almost no effort. They include massage machines, body wraps, coarse sea sponges, inflatable rubber clothes, sauna suits, and body creams, all claiming to "melt pounds away." The hundreds of diet formulas and potions include amino acid tablets, papaya-garlic pills, and Chinese tea diets.

The Food and Drug Administration (FDA) was set up to protect people from products that can be harmful to our health. Weight-loss gimmicks have certainly kept the FDA busy over the years, because many of these products not only don't work, but can actually harm their users. In 1983 the FDA seized 3.5 million dollars' worth of starch-blocking pills, which were supposed to block the digestion of carbohydrates. That same year they seized diet glasses that were supposed to make food look less attractive. Electric muscle stimulators claimed to be just as effective as running for hours, but they had no effect on weight loss and in fact could cause shocks or burns.

High-protein/low-carbohydrate diets may seem effective in many cases, but some studies have determined this type of diet can place a strain on the kidneys and can raise cholesterol and fat levels in the blood, increasing the risk of cardiovascular diseases. Reports of several deaths of people on such diets prompted the FDA to impose much stricter regulations on "liquid-protein" formulations.

Some diet plans insist that certain foods help burn calories by changing the body's metabolism. A grapefruit eaten before meals is supposed to help melt fat away, according to one diet. Doctors believe, however, that any weight loss due to these "metabolism changers" is merely due to the fact that the person is eating fewer calories.

Ten million Americans (mostly women) use diet pills that contain the amphetaminelike stimulant *phenylpropanolamine (PPA)*. However, some people may take more than the recommended amounts of drugs—and studies have shown that just twice the normal dose of PPA can increase the chances of high blood pressure, strokes, and seizures. PPA is also an ingredient in some cold and allergy remedies, which means that some people might be taking too much without realizing it. In addition, caffeine, when taken along with the drug, can increase the chances of harmful effects. Many medical experts believe that PPA should be available only by prescription, not over the counter.

Which Pounds to Lose?

When people go on a diet to lose weight, they want to lose the excess fat in their bodies. It is this extra fat that increases the possibility of health problems, and it's the fat that causes unsightly bulges in places we don't want them. But when a person goes on a diet, the body doesn't just burn up fat deposits. Some of the weight lost is body water. Research indicates that reduced-calorie diets also cause a loss of muscle tissue and of other organ tissue as well. Within twenty-four hours after a person fasts, for example, the body will begin to use muscle tissue as a source of energy. Dieting can cause heart tissue to be lost within six weeks after an obese person goes on even a moderate diet of 1,200 to 1,500 calories a day.

Ironically, the fewer calories the dieter takes in and the more muscle tissue that is lost, the harder it becomes to lose fat tissue. Muscle is a very metabolically active tissue, a heavy consumer of calories. A continuing intake of energy is needed to sustain it, which is not the case for fat tissue, which is just a storage depot. So as muscle tissue is lost, the body needs fewer calories to keep going.

For this and other reasons, doctors recommend that any weight-loss program be accompanied by regular exercise. Exercise increases muscle tissue and other "lean-body mass" (nonfat tissue). The overall effect of a combination of diet and exercise is weight loss without muscle loss. In one study, for example, one group of dieters ate 50 percent fewer calories and did not exercise. Another group reduced their calorie intake by only 25 percent but increased their physical activity by 25 percent. The group that only dieted lost more weight, but measurements showed that they lost fewer pounds of fat and more lean tissue than those who combined diet with exercise.

Unfortunately, most dieters do not exercise, and they may find they are damaging their bodies instead of improving their health.

If people realized just what dieting does to the body, there would probably be far fewer dieters. Some health officials would say that was for the better, considering the large numbers of people who diet when they do not really need to. However, there are many people who do need to lose weight for health reasons. For them it is important to find out what makes dieting so ineffective.

The Diet Yo-Yo

Most people who diet are trying to lose weight in a hurry—to get ready for the summer season, or to fit into the clothes they used to wear, or to make themselves "more attractive." These dieters find themselves continually going on crash diets—losing weight, then gaining it back, then going on another diet. Each time it seems easier to put the weight back on, and harder to take it off again. Doctors call this type of dieting *cycling* or *yo-yo dieting*. Some experts believe that yo-yo dieting actually can help contribute to obesity. Kelly Brownell, a psychologist at the University of Pennsylvania School of Medicine, describes a possible outcome of yo-yo dieting as "diet-induced obesity," because the dieting actually contributes to the person's obesity.

Dr. Brownell first studied yo-yo diets in rats. By regulating the amount of food they ate, he was able to plump the rats up and slim them down again. He noted how long it took the rats to gain a certain amount of weight, then he noted how long it took them to lose that amount of weight. When they were back to their original weight, the rats were fattened up again, and when they reached the level of fatness they had attained in the first cycle they were slimmed down again.

The rats took twenty-one days to lose the excess weight they had put on in the first cycle. In the second cycle, though, they took forty-six days to lose the same amount of weight, even though they were fed exactly the same amounts of food as in the first cycle. In addition, the researchers found that the rats gained weight much more quickly in the second plumping-up cycle. (It took only one third as long for the rats to regain the same amount of weight.)

Dr. Brownell believes that the rats' rate of metabolism was lowered, becoming more efficient, and the rats were able to maintain their body weight with fewer calories. But since they were given the same amount of food, they gained weight more quickly in the plumping stage, and they lost weight more slowly when they received less food because they no longer needed as many calories for their normal body functions.

Can we apply these findings to humans as well? The University of Pennsylvania researchers believe so. On the basis of the results in rats, a five-year study called the Weight Cycling Program was begun with human subjects, and the study revealed similar results.

High school and college wrestlers are prime examples of yo-yo dieters. Wrestlers often lose weight before matches to compete in lower weight classes. One study found that 41 percent of wrestlers lose between six and ten pounds per week. Forty-four percent reported losing between eleven and twenty pounds per week. Dr. Brownell noted that wrestlers whose weight fluctuated greatly did indeed have much lower metabolic rates than wrestlers whose weight did not fluctuate as much.

This lowering of the metabolic rate in the body may be the reason why many people give up their diets. Often dieters find they start to lose weight fairly quickly and easily, but then suddenly they can't seem to lose any more—they reach a plateau in which their weight stays constant even though they are still eating a reduced number of calories. This plateau is a safety mechanism built into our bodies. When the body seems to be facing starvation, the metabolic rate (BMR) falls drastically. Now the body needs less energy to continue functioning. Many people abandon their diets at this point, and soon they begin putting weight back on.

There are several other reasons that yo-yo dieters often find they gain even more weight than before they started dieting. Some studies have suggested that start-and-stop dieting actually changes the overall makeup of the body. Each time the person loses weight, fat and muscle are lost. But when the person goes back to normal eating patterns and gains weight again, most of the regained weight is fat. Thus the overall percentage of body fat increases. Each time the person diets, the percentage of fat goes up again.

Dr. Brownell suggests that a body enzyme might be the culprit here. Lipoprotein lipase (LPL) determines how much fat is stored in fat cells. Dieting causes LPL activity to increase, which results in more efficient storing of fat. Elevated LPL levels have been found to remain up to two years after an obese person has lost weight.

The LPL theory is supported by observations by Philip Kern and his associates at Cedars Sinai Medical Center in Los Angeles. A group of very obese people, who lost an average of ninety pounds each and maintained their new weight for three months, had higher LPL levels than before they dieted.

What's more, the fatter the people were originally, the higher their levels of the enzyme rose. The Cedars Sinai researchers found that activation of a gene in the fat cells was responsible for the increased LPL production.

Some research suggests that yo-yo dieting has an effect on food preferences. In one rat study, for example, cycling rats preferred fat over carbohydrates or proteins. Thus, a dieter who goes off his or her diet may then have a craving for more fattening foods, which soon restore the lost weight and make it all the harder to diet the next time.

Kelly Brownell believes that cyclical dieting may increase the risk of cardiovascular disease, as well, by stimulating the production of *low-density lipoproteins (LDLs)*, which promote the formation of cholesterol deposits inside artery walls. So for this reason, too, dieting could leave a person in worse health than before.

In 1985 the NIH declared that all Americans who weighed more than 20 percent more than their ideal weight should lose weight to lower their risks of numerous diseases. But the growing research on the hazards of yo-yo dieting have led some experts to believe that some overweight people might be better off not attempting to diet. John Brunzell at the University of Washington suggests that "normal obesity" might be a genetic condition that is inevitable in some people. Some studies seem to confirm this hypothesis with the finding that many patients seem to have normal metabolic rates while obese, but do not after losing weight.

Not all obesity studies have confirmed the results on cyclical dieting, and for the moment the debate continues.

MAKING
A DIET
WORK

MANY DIETS WORK, at least for a while. Dieters can lose weight, but studies have shown that 80 to 95 percent of dieters eventually regain most or all of the weight they lost. Some even put on more pounds than they have before. Still, some people are able to lose weight and keep it off. What's their secret?

Most weight experts agree that no crash diet or miracle pill, no magical gimmick will help a person take weight off and keep it off. The only diet that works is a complete change in eating habits—not just until you lose weight, but for the rest of your life.

"Diet for the rest of my life! Aaagh!"

One of the problems with the way we look at diets is that we see "diet" as a dirty word. It's only a desperate temporary change in our eating habits in an attempt to lose weight. Then, after we've lost the desired amount of weight, we can abandon our diet and go back to our old eating ways. That attitude is self-defeating. The key is to realize that everyone is on a diet. Our diet is simply the foods that we eat. Some diets are better than others. The ones that make us most healthy and still taste good are the best diets. In order to lose weight and keep it off, a person must change his or her eating habits *permanently*, to a new, healthier diet.

Plotting a Weight-Loss Plan

To even start a weight-loss diet, a person has to be motivated. It isn't just enough to have a desire to be thin. Motivation means you are willing to do whatever it takes to accomplish your goal of getting thinner and staying that way. You also need self-discipline. Dieting is not easy. There are so many temptations and discomforting cravings to overcome.

Once you've set your goal, you must realize that a successful diet is not a fast-acting diet. Experts suggest that you try to lose only one to two pounds per week. That doesn't seem like much at all, and the results after a day or two (or even a few weeks) may seem discouraging. But one pound a week can add up to fifty pounds in a year!

The next step is to learn about your nutritional needs, and to find an eating plan that will meet these needs—one that you will be able to live with.

Some people believe in high-protein diets, others in high-carbohydrate diets. But most experts agree that the best diet contains the normal recommended proportions of each group: protein, carbohydrates, and fats. While trying to lose weight, you just eat smaller portions of each. Then after you've lost the weight, you continue your "diet" eating larger portions of the same types of foods.

The only problem is that most modern people do not eat the proper proportions of food groups in their normal diet. The average American gets 42 percent of each day's calories from fat. About 66 percent of our calories come from high-fat and high-sugar foods, which also happen to be low in vitamins and minerals. Each day we eat an average of 400 calories of sugar (most of which come from sodas and other sugared drinks). This is a hundred pounds of sugar per year! These sugary and fatty foods either replace other healthier foods or are eaten in addition to other foods, which increase total calories and contribute to weight gain. So by choosing foods that are low in sugar and fats, we increase our chances of getting the right proportions of foods, and thus the healthiest diet.

We also do not eat enough fiber. Many experts believe that a high-fiber diet will not only be healthier but can actually help a person lose weight. High-fiber foods like fresh fruits and leafy vegetables, beans and peas, and whole-grain products, are naturally low in fat and high in vitamins and minerals. A person can eat more fiber foods, thus feeling fuller, but get fewer calories than fatty foods supply.

Studies have found that when people consciously try to cut down on sugary and fatty foods, they end up eating more grains, fruits, and vegetables, as well as other foods that provide the vitamins and minerals they had been missing.

Often the foods we eat are not bad at all for us, but the way we prepare them makes them less healthy. Baked chicken without the skin, for example, has less than half as many calories as the same-size piece of chicken fried. A baked potato's calories can double or triple with margarine or sour cream on top.

Dieters may have another reason to stay away from fatty foods. Some researchers believe that all calories are not the same. Not only does fat contain more calories, gram for gram, than carbohydrates and proteins, but according to Robert E. Stark, president of the American Society of Bariatric Physicians (who specialize in treating overweight people), "97 percent of all fat calories are converted to body fat." According to Dr. Stark, carbohydrates and proteins, on the contrary, have to be consumed in large quantities before the body converts any of them to body fat. Studies have found that people on diets of only 1,500 calories gained weight when 50 percent of those calories came from fat.

You can calculate the percentage of fat in foods by reading labels that list the grams of fat and the total calories per portion. Multiply the grams of fat by nine (the number of calories in one gram of fat). That will tell you how many calories come from fat. Then divide that number by the total number of calories to find out the percentage of calories from fat. Remember, doctors recommend that no more than 30 percent of the calories in a healthy diet should come from fat. A helpful list of 1,200 common foods with the percentage of fat in each of them is provided in a booklet by Dr. Robert Stark, called *The % Fat Calorie Tables* (available from the Arizona Bariatric Physicians, P.C., 444 W. Osborn Rd., Phoenix AZ 85013).

Keeping a "food diary" before you begin your diet can be a real eye-opener. You should note not only what foods you eat, and when, but also the size of the portions (actually weigh them—people normally tend to underestimate how much they eat) and the circumstances in which they were eaten. You may discover, for example, that you tend to munch snacks while watching TV or reading. Perhaps your typical reaction to feeling upset is to reach for a candy bar or raid the refrigerator for leftovers. You may think you are eating wisely but are really fooling yourself by little rationalizations—saving 30 calories or so by using an artificial sweetener instead of sugar, for example, and then figuring you're ahead for the day so you can splurge on a chocolate mousse dessert. (You can't fool your body; your metabolism counts every single calorie you take in.) The food diary will give you a more realistic idea of how much you are actually eating and may provide clues to ways you can cut back almost painlessly.

A recent review of diet programs in *Hippocrates* magazine suggests a quick way to figure out how many calories you really need, and how far you can safely cut back in a weight-loss effort. Multiply the weight you would like to be by the appropriate one of the following numbers:

For women:
10 if you are sedentary (you do some walking but no heavy exercise);
13 if you are moderately active (exercise three times a week);
15 if you are very active (run, swim, or engage in other forms of vigorous exercise nearly every day).

For men:
13 if you are sedentary;
15 if you are moderately active;
20 if you are very active.

If your target weight is 125 pounds, for example, and you are a moderately active woman, you need $125 \times 13 = 1{,}625$ calories a day to maintain the weight you'd like to be.

If you are heavier than you'd like and want to lose weight, cut down what you are currently eating by 500 calories a day to lose one pound a week, or more if you want to lose faster. But experts advise that you should not aim to lose more than two to three pounds a week—at that rate your body can adjust to the change. The experts also say that you shouldn't cut your food intake below 1,100 to 1,200 calories a day; less than that amount of food can deprive you of needed vitamins and minerals and leave you feeling sluggish and grouchy—more likely to give up the diet.

When you reach your goal, adjust your daily diet to the number of calories corresponding to your target weight and level of activity.

Diet Tactics

The total number of calories eaten and the proportions of fats, carbohydrates, and proteins in the diet are not the whole story. The timing of meals can also play an important role in dieting success. One mistake that people often make is to skip meals, figuring that they are saving a whole meal's worth of calories that way. But skipping meals can trigger the body's starvation warning signals. You will feel hungrier later and may eat more than you intended when you do have a meal. Moreover, making a habit of meal skipping may trigger a slowdown of body metabolism. Skipping breakfast is particularly bad, since the body has gone all night without an intake of nutrients and fluids. A good breakfast can start the day right and should contain substantial amounts of protein and starchy carbohydrates. (Sugary breakfast foods may be taste-tempting, but they can stimulate the appetite.)

Eating the larger meals early in the day (the opposite of our typical American pattern) takes advantage of the higher metabolic rate while we are up and active. Heavy bedtime snacks are one of the worst things a dieter can do—digestion and absorption of the food occur while the body metabolism is turned down for sleep; few calories are burned off, and the excess is stored away as fat.

Some nutritionists say that even our traditional three meals a day are too few. For a healthy weight-loss program they recommend splitting the day's food intake into a number of small meals— perhaps five or six—spread over the waking day. The dieter who uses this approach takes advantage of a metabolic bonus called the *thermic response*. This is a rise in the metabolic rate after eating, due mostly to the increase in energy needed to eat and digest food. Researchers believe that 10 percent of the calories in food are burned up in this thermic response. By eating many small meals, you jump-start your metabolism many times a day. There is a danger, though. The key is to divide the same total amount of food into a larger number of meals, but many dieters, used to eating a few big meals, do not feel satisfied by the smaller "snacks" and wind up taking second helpings and actually eating more calories over the course of the day.

If you are trying to lose weight by eating smaller portions of your normal, balanced diet, there are some tricks that can help you feel more satisfied and make it easier to stick to the reduced calorie intake. Measure out the portions beforehand,

and don't leave serving dishes on the table where it is convenient to take second helpings. Using smaller dishes can make those smaller portions look larger and help you to feel you are getting "enough." Try new, low-calorie recipes to help satisfy your food urges with variety rather than quantity. Eat slowly and chew thoroughly; each meal should last from twenty to thirty minutes. It takes time—up to twenty minutes—for the signals of "fullness" to register in the brain, and if you bolt your food in a few minutes, you will still feel hungry when you have finished. When you eat, always sit down and eat your food on a plate. Don't stand in front of the refrigerator nibbling—you'll probably end up eating more than you intended.

Get rid of the high-calorie foods and snacks in your refrigerator and cabinets, and buy only what you intend to eat on your diet. (If the food isn't handy, you are much less likely to yield to a sudden urge.) Avoid packaged snack foods, because they are usually high in fat. (Two ounces of potato chips contain 320 calories, but four cups of popcorn, made without oil or butter, have only 100 calories.) Eat baked, broiled, or poached foods instead of fried foods, and cut down further on fats by substituting skim milk and low-fat dairy products for the regular kinds. (A cup of whole milk contains 150 calories, but a cup of skim milk has only 85.)

Salt can be a key ingredient in the diet, even though it contains no calories, because it increases water retention. Eating less food means that less salt is taken into the body. This decrease in the body's salt level causes diuresis, an increase in the amount of fluids going through the kidneys and being excreted in the urine. Some dieters decide if they can't have much food, they want flavor and add extra salt to their foods. But this will cause water retention and bring disappointment when the dieter steps on the scale.

Almost everyone on any reducing diet loses

weight at the beginning—up to six pounds in the first week. Most of this is water weight. Soon the BMR drops, though, and it's harder to lose weight. Often, after about three weeks of dieting, the person hits a plateau. He or she just can't lose any more weight. This is when most dieters give up their diets. An increase in exercise, however, can conquer the plateau problem. It will raise the BMR, and the weight loss will resume.

Why Dieters Fail

Nearly one in three dieters find their diets sabotaged by their family or close friends, often unintentionally. People may say or do things that make dieters feel they are not making progress, or don't need to diet. At parties and other social gatherings, overeating is often encouraged. It's important to learn to say "No, thank you."

There are many other reasons why dieters give up dieting. Some are overwhelmed by the constant temptation. Although eating disorders have much in common with substance addictions such as alcoholism or drug dependence, you can't quit a food dependence "cold turkey." Abstinence is not an option for overeaters—their lives literally depend on learning to eat in moderation. Counselors compare drinking alcohol to a lion you must keep in a cage. That is hard enough, but if you are an overeater, you must walk your lion three times a day!

Experts believe some of the main reasons for dieting failure are self-defeating attitudes and unrealistic expectations. Most people want to see results fast—but they usually expect faster results than are safely possible. They may think that once they lose that extra weight, their lives will suddenly fall into place; but life is rarely so simple.

One of the biggest reasons for quitting a diet is the feeling of frustration and defeat when a dieter slips and eats something he or she shouldn't have. Diets become like rituals, and when the routine is broken, it's easy to regard the lapse as an unforgivable sin. Doctors call this "dietary failure syndrome." The dieter thinks, "Well, I went off the diet, so what I do now doesn't matter"—and goes on a binge, eating hundreds or thousands of extra calories. A binge like that can quickly undo all the hard-won progress and put the weight back on.

What to Do When You Slip

If you're going to be serious about your new diet, you have to realize that occasionally you'll make a mistake. If you turn it into a learning experience, then you haven't lost anything. There's always another day. By continuing to keep a food diary of everything you eat, you can help keep yourself on the right track. Knowing that you are going to write down on paper everything you put in your mouth often makes you think twice before eating something you shouldn't. Then red circles around the food slip-ups remind you to watch out for those tempting items.

Dr. Alan Marlatt at the University of Washington urges weight reducers to carry a card around with them that lists a six-step plan to help keep slipups from turning into relapses.

---

1. **When** you make a slipup, stop and remove yourself from the situation.
2. Immediately remind yourself that a slip doesn't mean you're a failure.
3. Renew your decision to lose weight,

and remind yourself how far you've already come.

4. Go over in your mind what caused the slip. Identify the "trigger factors" so that you will be able to overcome them next time.

5. Take an action that you previously had planned to do in case this happens—take a walk, for example, or get rid of the rest of the food.

6. Get help from someone else if you need more support to avoid a relapse.

The families of dieters should try to be encouraging, and tolerant when slipups occur.

The dieter should develop some standard techniques for coping with temptation. Many people believe that giving in to an urge will make it feel better. Actually, though, it makes the urges come more often and strongly. If you try distracting yourself by doing something else when urges come, they will pass and become less urgent and less frequent. Cravings usually last for about twenty minutes and then subside, whether or not we eat. If you can keep yourself busy even for a few minutes when cravings begin, often they will pass. Take a shower, knit, read a book, write a letter, look at photo albums, or work on a hobby—do something constructive that will take your mind off food. Taking a walk is one of the best distractions, because in addition to getting away from food you're getting exercise, which helps burn off calories. When the hunger pangs or food cravings hit, try sipping a glass of water. (Often we misinterpret our bodies' signals, and a vague discomfort that we think is hunger may actually be prompted by thirst.) If you feel you just have to eat to satisfy an uncontrollable craving, snack on fruits, raw vegetables, or unbuttered popcorn instead of potato chips or cookies.

More Tips for Success

Keeping a log listing the amount of weight you lose can help to give you a feeling of progress and prop up your motivation when you are tempted to slip. But some weight-loss experts advise that you weigh yourself only once or twice a week at the most, at the same time of day with the same amount of clothing. The normal body weight can fluctuate more than two pounds during the day because of variations in water weight. Most dieters like to see improvements every time they get on the scale, and too-frequent weighing will only lead to disappointment. If you do get discouraged, look at your log to see how far you've already come.

Dining out can be a dieter's downfall, but it doesn't have to be. According to Darlene Dougherty of the American Dietetic Association, the biggest problem when dieters dine out is the "clean plate syndrome." We think we have to eat everything on our plates. (The feeling may be a carryover from childhood, when we were cautioned not to waste food and encouraged to "eat up so you'll grow big and strong." There is also the desire to seem polite and not appear unappreciative of a host or hostess.) Get into the habit of leaving some food on the plate. Don't be bashful about apologizing gracefully, "This is so delicious—I wish my diet would let me eat more of it!" (Chances are good that your host or hostess has dieted too, and can sympathize with you.) In a restaurant, you can ask for a doggy bag for the leftovers. (They may make a tasty meal for the following day.) Drink low-fat milk with meals instead of sugary sodas. Fill up on vegetables at the salad bar. (But watch out for high-calorie items like potato salad with mayonnaise.) Think about bringing serving-size containers of low-calorie salad dressings with you. Split an entrée—or a dessert—with someone.

Remember that negative feelings of depression and frustration are normal for people on a diet, but don't wallow in them. **Remind yourself that you're not dieting, you've just chosen a healthier way to eat.** Most experts believe that if you really do change your eating habits, it's okay to occasionally have that special treat you miss—but only once in a while, and only in small portions. When you go to parties, save room for a little splurging by eating less during the day, and exercise more to burn off any extra calories you might eat. (But remember that "good-tasting" foods often have a *lot* of calories—you would have to run for two hours to burn off the calories in a candy bar!) During the party, try talking to more people so that you have less time to eat.

It's not easy to stay on a diet, but most people who lose weight and keep it off feel better about themselves, and they will be much healthier, besides.

Keeping it off, though—that can be an even bigger problem than taking weight off in the first place. Even if the dieter successfully fights the continual temptations to go back to "normal" eating patterns after the target weight has been reached, his or her body may adjust to the new, lower-calorie norm and begin to metabolize food more efficiently. Then the pounds may begin to creep back on. Over the long term, there are the gradual effects of ageing: A person's metabolism tends to slow down by 2 percent for each decade of life. Gradually, despite all that willpower and heroic self-denial, the body loses muscle and gains fat.

Is it hopeless, then? Is dieting a losing game and the dieter doomed to failure?

Not necessarily. Fortunately, there is another powerful weapon in the fight against fat—one that works on a long-term basis and can help to improve not only appearance but fitness and health as well. That weapon is exercise.

BURN
IT OFF

TO GAIN WEIGHT, a person has to eat more calories than his or her body uses. So it's only natural to assume that one of the major causes of obesity is overeating. Many experts, however, such as William Haskell, a physiologist at Stanford University's medical school, believe that not overeating but rather lack of exercise "is the major culprit in the weight gain most Americans are faced with."

Many more people today lead sedentary lives than was the case in previous times. Modern jobs typically require much less physical activity than the jobs of a few decades ago. At home, television watching is one of America's favorite pastimes, and "couch potatoes" seem almost proud of their inactivity. Eating snacks often goes hand in hand with watching TV, which can only contribute to weight problems.

Television watching has long been suspected of contributing to obesity. Now studies are finding that it may lead to deteriorating muscles, as well. In a study of high school boys, those who watched less TV did much better in a series of fitness tests. In another study, mentioned in Chapter 6, 40 percent of boys age six to seventeen and 70 percent of girls in the same age group couldn't do more than one pull-up. Thirty percent of boys and 50 percent of girls couldn't run a mile in less than ten minutes. In all the tests of physical strength and endurance, young people of today had poorer scores than kids of the past. This trend has health experts concerned, and they believe TV has a lot to do with it.

The Fitness Fad

It's not as though Americans aren't health conscious. The country has been caught up in a fitness fad that has lasted for over ten years. One survey found that twenty-five million Americans begin exercising for the first time each year. Another poll discovered that more than half of all Americans exercise regularly. In his 1987 book *Inside America*, poll taker Louis Harris reported that 75 percent of Americans claimed they exercise regularly. One third claimed they worked out vigorously three times a week. The sales of athletic equipment certainly seem to confirm these claims. Americans spend over eight billion dollars a year on athletic equipment. Seven million Americans pay five billion dollars each year for membership fees to health and fitness clubs.

At the same time, Americans have been caught up in a diet craze as well. One third of all foods bought in this country are low-calorie foods—over seventy-four billion dollars' worth. Louis Harris found that 59 percent of Americans claimed they "try hard" to eat more fiber, and 46 percent avoid high-cholesterol foods.

And yet, with all of these claims, most experts believe there are more overweight people in America than ever. Many people have good intentions about exercising and dieting, but they may not always live up to their goals. According to one study, for example, four out of five people with jogging shoes jog less than once a week, and more than half don't even jog once a year! Half of all bicycle owners don't bicycle, and half of all those who own weight-lifting equipment almost never use it!

Louis Harris found that steak, ham, and roast beef were the most popular entrées at restaurants, far outdistancing lower-cholesterol and lower-calorie choices. Many people do eat lower-calorie products, but one problem is that many people seem to think that these products will whisk away their excess weight. Exercise is not a part of most dieters' weight-loss programs.

Some reseachers, like *American Demographics* associate editor Joe Schwartz, think that polls and studies often reflect a typical human tendency: People tend to answer the way they think they should, the way they would ideally like to act, or the way they believe they act, not necessarily the way they really do act. People may have noble intentions, but they forget all the little times they didn't follow their plans. They may intend, for example, to exercise three times a week, but one day something comes up, another day they may work late—and before you know it, that three times a week turns into one day of exercise or less. The same thing can happen with a diet. A pastry here, a roast beef sandwich there . . . If a person doesn't keep track of everything he or she actually eats, it is very hard to see that each of those little "extras" can add up to a lot of calories.

Another reason there may be so many overweight people is that until recently it seemed that most of the people who were exercising were already in fairly good shape. According to some psychologists, overweight people may have tended to exercise less because the media portrayed exercisers as fit young people doing strenuous activities. The overweight have difficulty identifying with that kind of image, and they had the impression that the exercises pictured were beyond their abilities—so they never really got started. Expressions like "No pain, no gain" made any benefits from exercise seem much too hard to work for.

But in the 1980s health officials declared that any type of exercise—even common chores like mowing the lawn, working in the garden, and doing housework—can help improve our cardiovascular, muscular, and digestive systems and our overall health. A study of seventeen thousand Harvard graduates found that regular exercise reduced the risk of dying from every major disease. Dr. Roy K. Shepard has found that exercise can be beneficial even for the elderly. Older people who exercise regularly for a year will feel ten years younger.

Now a new twist in the fitness trend is for obese people to become involved, not necessarily to control their weight, but to improve their health and feel better about themselves. The number of exercise classes for overweight people has skyrocketed. New lines of clothing and accessories for the overweight, permitting them to dress comfortably and fashionably while exercising, have helped to encourage this trend.

Exercise and Weight Loss

Exercise by itself is not a very good way to lose weight. Calories are burned off very slowly. Walking burns off only five calories per minute. Marathon runners who run twenty-six miles lose only three quarters of a pound of fat in their grueling run of over two hours. These numbers may seem disappointingly small. It would take eleven hours of walking, for example, or seven hours of bicycling to lose just one pound. But remember that the effects of exercise add up, day after day. Grant Gwinup, an endocrinologist at the University of California at Irvine, has found that walking or bicycling for at least thirty minutes a day results in weight loss even without dieting. (Half an hour of walking a day can take off nearly seventeen pounds in a year, and a daily half hour of bicycling could result in the loss of twenty-six pounds in a year.)

According to Loren Greene, clinical assistant professor of medicine at the New York University Medical Center, exercise is a good way for someone to start a weight-loss program. It helps build up motivation and commitment to getting in better shape. But, Dr. Greene points out, exercise only works in helping to lose weight and keeping it off when it is accompanied by a lower intake of calories. (It takes thirty-seven minutes of walking, for example, just to work off the calories in a small serving of ice cream.) Studies have found that many who start with an exercise program and stick to it begin to practice better eating habits after a while.

Exercise works well with a reduced-calorie diet for many reasons. Exercise provides a psychological boost for those who want to lose weight. It helps raise a dieter's self-esteem, which helps provide motivation to stick to the diet. Exercise helps relieve tension (including the stress and depression that dieting may produce) and makes a person feel better both physically and mentally. Exercising regularly has been shown to reduce the heart rate and lower blood pressure, in addition to helping the heart pump more effectively. Moderate exercise may also have an appetite-suppressing effect, making it easier to stick to a diet; while burning off calories, it promotes the loss of fat rather than muscle tissue. University of Washington medical school endocrinologist Scott Weigle believes that exercising also gives people "something to focus on besides food."

Although nearly all obesity experts agree that increased exercise must accompany any diet program, there is a lot of controversy over many of the claims about exercise and weight loss. One of the biggest debates is focused on how exercise affects the body's metabolism.

As we have seen, many experts believe that during dieting the body's metabolism becomes more efficient, and fewer calories are needed to maintain normal activities. Eventually the dieter reaches a plateau, where no more weight is lost even though the food intake is still low. If the dieter does not become discouraged and give up, after a while he or she will begin to lose weight again. When exercise is combined with dieting, it helps overcome these plateaus more quickly.

There is a good deal of evidence that exercise not only burns off calories *during* the physical activity but also speeds up the person's metabolism for some time afterward. Thus the body continues to burn off more fat during these periods than it would have without exercise. Some research has found that after half an hour of exercise, the body may burn up to 20 percent more calories for the next two to four hours! Other experts say the metabolism is elevated for only half an hour at the most.

This disagreement may be due at least partly to differences in the kind and amount of exercise in the different studies, and to the effects of the subjects' physical condition. Researchers believe that the body's metabolism tries to adapt to maintain a constant body weight despite changes in the amount of food and exercise we do from day to day. When inactive people exercise, the body has not yet adjusted to the change in activity, and the increased activity causes the body to burn up calories as muscles use energy to perform. But exercise does not affect moderately active people as much. (Active people don't get out of breath as quickly as inactive people, for example.) Professional athletes, though, do have increased metabolism after exercise because they have so much muscle tissue. Muscle is very active metabolically, and muscles require a lot of energy both during exercise and to maintain them between exercise sessions.

Recent studies by British researchers suggest that some people may be naturally less physically active than others—and also more inclined to be overweight—because of hereditary differences in their muscle fibers. The scientists found that muscles contain various proportions of *"slow" fibers*, which use fatty acids for energy, and *"fast" fibers*, which use glucose as their fuel. People whose muscles contain more fast fibers tire more easily when they exercise and tend to be fatter than those with a larger proportion of slow fibers.

Another controversy about exercise and weight

loss concerns whether exercise makes a person hungrier or helps to curb a person's appetite. Many studies have found that overweight people eat less when they exercise regularly. But others insist this is not necessarily so. David Levitsky, a nutrition scientist at Cornell University, explains, "Exercising causes a depletion in glycogen, the muscles' fuel, which must be replaced. While there's a temporary decrease in appetite immediately after exertion, the truth is the more you exercise, over a period of time, the more you eat." However, fat tissue is lost and muscle tissue is gained through exercise—even with this increased appetite.

Other researchers have found that the appetite-control mechanism in obese people does not work properly, which may cause them to eat more than normal. According to one theory, obese people may have a reduced sensitivity to insulin, the hormone secreted by the pancreas when the blood sugar level is high. Their body cells may not respond to insulin in the normal way, by taking up sugar from the blood and converting it to energy. More insulin is secreted and stimulates the brain's appetite center—so the person continues to feel hungry. Researchers have found, however, that regular exercise can help raise insulin sensitivity and normalize the body's sugar levels.

What Kind of Exercise Program?

An obese person of any age should not begin an exercise program or a strict weight-loss program of any kind without consulting a doctor, especially if the person has any kind of health problems. Continuous, rhythmic activity, which health specialists refer to as *aerobic exercise*, puts stress on many body structures but also the heart and lungs, which help to supply the body cells with the oxygen and food substances they need. Working muscles consume large amounts of sugar and oxygen, and the heart action speeds up during exercise to pump more blood to the muscles. The pulse rate may thus increase from a normal 70 or so to 120, 150, or even more beats per minute. The maximum rate that the heart can safely achieve without damaging stress depends on a person's age and general physical condition. After the preexercise examination, the doctor can suggest what percentage of the maximum heart rate would be best for a particular individual to work up to.

For years people have been told that good exercise should be done at 70 to 80 percent of a person's top heart rate. But now researchers are finding that moderate exercise, bringing the pulse rate up to 40 to 50 percent of the maximum, can burn just as much fat. *Low-impact aerobics*, in which one foot is always on the floor, is a popular way of exercising moderately. Forty-five million Americans are now walking as part of their exercise plan. Most types of exercise are good—whatever you *like* to do—as long as the routine can fit easily into your schedule and not cause too much pain. It's important to develop that exercise program into a lifelong habit. Some suggest that one way to do this is to exercise at the same time every day. After a while the day doesn't feel complete unless you've exercised.

To figure out your maximum aerobic capacity, subtract your age from 220. Then, depending on whether your doctor suggests that exercising be done at 40, 50, 60, 70, or 80 percent of your maximum pulse rate, you simply multiply by .40, .50, .60, .70, or .80 to find the pulse rate you should aim for during exercise.

Overweight people often become overheated

very quickly. In warm weather, it is best to wear light, loose clothing, and to exercise in a well-ventilated place. (Exercising in a heavy sweatsuit or with plastic wraps around "problem areas" promotes sweating—a loss of body water, not body fat.) The pulse rate should also be checked often to make sure one is not overdoing it. You should drink water before, during, and after exercising.

Most health experts suggest that overweight people stick to low-impact aerobic exercises to reduce the chance of injury to the back and legs. Swimming and water aerobics are often suggested for those who are out of shape, because there is much less chance of injury. Overweight people who are very out of shape should begin with simple stretching exercises before they move up to aerobic exercises.

Not all exercises are good for you. Some are fine for people who are in top shape, but some of the traditional exercises can strain muscles, according to a report by the International Dance-Exercise Association. They published a list of contra-indicated exercises, which can be harmful for some people.

According to the report, sit-ups should be done

with the legs bent; keeping them straight during this exercise can cause lower-back problems. Leg lifts can also cause lower-back problems. Deep knee bends are not good for the knees. Quick full neck circles can cause neck injuries. Only slow half circles or side-to-side motions are recommended. When doing push-ups, you should be careful not to arch your back. Even toe touches can put unnecessary strain on the spine. The report also suggests that it is dangerous to develop only one group of muscles in an area, because this can lead to imbalance and often causes one muscle group to become overtired as well. In general, if an exercise causes discomfort, it may need to be modified.

Although charts might indicate that swimming is one of the best ways to burn off calories, one study conducted by Grant Gwinup of the University of California found that moderately overweight subjects who walked and bicycled without dieting lost weight, but those who swam *gained* weight! The researchers believe that swimming may cause the body to retain fat as a way of insulating against heat loss. Thirty times more heat is lost from the skin in water than in air.

Those who believe that exercise increases

the metabolism suggest that exercising several
times a day for shorter periods is more effective than a single long session. For example, if
you exercise for an hour and a half a day, you could
do it in two forty-five-minute sessions, or three
thirty-minute sessions. Researchers have found that
the three sessions burn twice as much body fat.
Every time you exercise, the body metabolism
speeds up, then it returns to a normal level. The
more times you speed up the metabolism, the more
fat is burned.

People tend to measure their progress in a
weight-loss program by periodically checking
their weight. This approach can be misleading,
though. Exercise promotes the loss of fat while
conserving (or even increasing) muscle tissue. But
muscle is heavier than fat—so someone who is
losing weight by diet alone may lose pounds
much faster than a person on a combined program
of diet and exercise. The dieter who is exercising
is actually in much better shape—looks better and
feels better, too. For this reason, some experts
suggest that instead of, or at least in addition to,
taking weekly weight measurements, the dieter
should measure girth (the distance around key

body parts, such as the chest, waist, hips, upper arms, and thighs), as well. **Inches lost, rather than pounds lost, are a much better indication of fat loss.**

GETTING HELP

IN THE FALL of 1987, Walter Hudson had an accident. On his way to the bathroom he fell and then discovered he was wedged tight in his bedroom doorway. His family tried to help, but they couldn't get him out. It took firemen, police, and the county emergency team more than four hours to get Hudson unstuck and back into his bed. At forty-two, he was suffering from various ailments including headaches, backaches, breathing problems, and arthritis, but those were not the reasons for all the difficulty. "I was addicted to food," says Hudson, and his compulsive eating had made him the heaviest man in the world. (Experts think he weighed about twelve hundred pounds at the time, but no one is sure. When three weightlifters helped him up onto a special scale with a capacity of a thousand pounds, he broke the scale!) Provided for by Social Security disability checks and the care of a loving family, he had been outside only once in the past twenty-five years.

When Hudson's story hit the headlines, offers of help came in from all over the world. Self-taught nutritionist Dick Gregory put Hudson on a carefully supervised diet. By Christmas he had lost more than three hundred pounds, and as the weight loss continued he spoke hopefully of getting down to about 190 within a few years. "I want to feel the rain on my face," he said, "and to see my mother's grave." He wanted to get out and see the changes in the world that he had missed, perhaps marry one day, and help others who have eating problems.

Cases of obesity as extreme as Walter Hudson's are very rare, but growing numbers of people are seeking help for eating problems.

Some studies have found that the number of people who consider themselves overweight has not changed that much in recent years. But 75 percent of those questioned in the past believed they could diet successfully on their own. In a recent study, only 60 percent of the women who considered themselves overweight thought they could handle the problem on their own. This is one reason why so many people are seeking help from diet services.

The diet industry has skyrocketed. Americans spend billions of dollars on diet services. Not only women but also men are now becoming concerned and reaching for help.

At one time, the only help an overweight person could get was from small groups of friends who gathered together to share their experiences and help one another to lose weight. Today the overweight person looking for help can choose from thousands of weight-loss centers and programs around the country.

There are several main types of diet services. Liquid diet programs, such as Optifast, can be found at liquid diet centers, in hospitals, and in doctors' private practices. In the residential programs, sometimes called "fat farms" or "longevity centers," a person stays at the program's location for a week to six months or longer. Drop-in weight-loss centers provide various combinations of diet and exercise programs and group counseling. Finally, support groups such as Overeaters Anonymous furnish a mutual support system for people struggling with food addictions.

Hype or Help?

The diet industry has become a big business. Many programs sell packaged foods and food supplements to make following the program easier. This has some nutritionists and health experts up in arms. Morton H. Maxwell, codirector of UCLA's Risk Factor Obesity Program, for example, believes that some of the programs have become nothing more than glorified grocery stores. He also feels that the "trained" counselors in some of the programs do not have the proper training to give sound nutritional advice.

But for many people who have tried dieting on their own, these services may offer the only chance of losing weight. Studies have shown that about 95 percent of those who try dieting on their own regain most of the weight they lost within a year. In most good weight-loss programs, 85 percent of those participating will lose weight during the pro-

gram, and 50 percent will be able to keep that
weight off for a year or more after the program is
over.

Not all the programs available offer the same
services, and not all the programs are effective for
all people. Many offer nutritional counseling (either on a daily or weekly basis), exercise instruc-
tion, and special nutritional foods and supplements.
One program even has a squad of Diet Cops who
make unannounced checkups on dieters at their
homes to make sure they are sticking to their diets.

Medical experts warn dieters to avoid programs
that offer quick results. These usually involve extremely low-calorie diets and can cause a lot of
muscle tissue loss. There can be many harmful side
effects such as swollen joints, dizziness, muscle
cramps, anemia, and lowered immunity that leave
the dieter vulnerable to colds and other illnesses.

Experts warn against programs based on fad
diets that stress one particular food or food group;
they suggest that the safest and most effective programs are based on a balanced diet of a variety of
regular foods that are high in carbohydrates and
low in fats and supply at least 800 to 1,000 calories
per day. (Any diet with calorie intake at these low

levels must be monitored by a physician!) The effective programs encourage regular exercise, teach participants about nutrition, and use *behavior-modification* techniques; they promote losing weight slowly and are monitored by a dietician and or doctor. Finally, they stress the objective of maintaining weight loss, not just taking the weight off.

Behavior Modification

Behavior-modification tactics are a key part of many diet programs. The underlying idea is that eating problems are a learned behavior, and so they can be unlearned, and new, healthier behaviors can be substituted for them.

There are several elements common to most behavior-modification therapies:

- **Self-monitoring:** A diet diary, as described in Chapter 9, helps the person identify the times and places and reasons that contribute to unwanted eating behaviors.
- **Substituting good foods for bad ones:** Most behavior-modification pro-

grams involve substituting low-fat foods for the high-fat foods that the dieter normally ate.

- **Controlling the way we eat:** Various devices such as counting the number of chews per bite, or putting down the knife and fork between bites, are often employed to slow down eating.

- **Controlling cues that cause unwanted eating behaviors:** This may consist of keeping high-calorie foods out of sight, or being allowed to eat only in specific places and at specific times.

- **Change in attitude:** Often people fall into negative thought patterns that cause lack of self-esteem and result in abandoning a diet. Behavior modification seeks to show them new ways of looking at situations.

- **Rewards for success:** Good behaviors are rewarded with nonfood rewards, like new clothes or a movie. These good behaviors can be losing weight or controlling tempting situations or behaviors.

• **The importance of exercise as a new way of life:** Exercise programs are now becoming an important part of establishing a new, healthier way to live.

Behavior-modification programs achieve weight loss slower than traditional diets, but studies have found that when the program is over, patients continue to practice the new behavior patterns and keep weight off longer. Doctors consider this the best approach for moderately overweight people.

Drop-in Diet Centers

One of the oldest and most popular weight-loss programs is Weight Watchers. The program offers behavior modification, group psychological counseling, exercise, and weekly weigh-ins, in addition to prepackaged foods that are available in almost every supermarket. (The special foods are recommended but are not essential for following the Weight Watchers program.) There are more than fifteen thousand Weight Watchers meetings every week in twenty-four countries around the world.

In 1988 one million people attended meetings each week, and an estimated twenty-five million people have attended Weight Watchers meetings.

There are several other popular drop-in diet centers. Diet Center has twenty-three hundred locations in the United States and in Canada. There are three hundred Jenny Craig Weight Loss Centers and twelve hundred Nutri/System programs. Family Weight Loss Centers and Take Off Pounds Sensibly (TOPS) are also popular programs.

Liquid Diet Programs

Liquid weight-loss programs are enjoying another surge of popularity. With celebrity success stories like Oprah Winfrey's weight loss, many people are turning to these extremely low-calorie, doctor-supervised diets. For example, 650,000 dieters have joined Optifast's twenty-six-week liquid diet program.

Some doctors offer programs using liquid diets for their patients who wish to lose weight. Many hospital programs around the country have diet programs, and many of these include a liquid diet.

Typically, hospital programs start with a fasting period in which the patient receives only a low-calorie liquid diet under medical supervision. The next stage is a "refeeding" stage, in which the patient eats low-calorie solids along with the liquid. The last stage is the "stabilization" stage, when patients establish a new, healthier lifelong diet to help keep the lost weight off. Other hospital programs offer psychotherapy, behavior modification, and exercise under the supervision of doctors, psychologists, nutritionists, and physical therapists.

The long-term benefits of liquid-diet programs are controversial, and there have not been any well-documented follow-up studies. After a person completes the supervised program, the intense commitment tends to drop off, and old eating habits may be reestablished. (Even Oprah, under the watchful eyes of millions of TV viewers, gradually gained back part of the weight she had lost on the Optifast program.)

Hundreds of other doctor-supervised weight-loss clinics that use liquid diets, behavior modification, and numerous other tactics have sprung up all over. Even hypnosis is being used by some doctors for treating moderately overweight people. Since the brain is the source of the body's feeling of fullness, some believe that hypnosis can be used to focus a person's attention on the feeling of fullness, and often to produce that feeling. In one experiment at Stanford, a woman under hypnosis imagined she was eating a meal. After forty-five minutes she declared, "Let's stop, I'm full."

Residential Programs

For some people a residential program is the only answer. Dieters can spend a week, or a month, or longer at a residential program's facility, whether in a hospital or at a private center. There are all kinds of programs available, from Pritikin's longevity centers that stress changes in life-style to promote better health, to Kempner's Rice Diet program in North Carolina, where dieters eat rice and fruit for three to four months.

Psychological Counseling

Many compulsive eating problems stem from a distorted body image. People may blame the problems in their lives on the things they don't like about their bodies. Compulsive overeating gets worse and worse with yo-yo dieting. Anorexia and bulimia arise when people continue to see themselves as fat even when they aren't. For this reason, many experts believe an important approach to overcoming abnormal eating behaviors is to go to the root of the problem at a psychological level. They believe that people need to discover why they don't like the way they are, and to learn to like their bodies.

To help people gain a better sense of judgment about their bodies, how they really are, and what is really the best shape and weight for the individual, experts use various techniques. One is an approach called *mirroring* or *visualization*. For many years athletes like Olympic gold-medal winner Mary Lou Retton have been using this technique to make themselves perform better. Mirroring can be an important way to build up the confidence of a person who needs to lose weight and stick to a change in diet.

Sculpting is one visualization technique developed by psychotherapist Fran Weiss, as part of a plan to help women discover the causes of distorted self-perceptions. Dr. Weiss helps the patient set specific high and low limits—which weights are desirable and which weights aren't. Then doctor and patient explore what benefits will be obtained if the desired weight is reached. The positive role of fat in the body is also explored, so that the patient realizes that not all fat is bad.

Dr. Weiss and other psychotherapists use various visualization techniques in their therapies. One technique is to have the patient draw portraits of what she thinks she looks like to various people in her life. The therapist can then determine where conflicts might lie. Then the patient stands in front of a three-sided mirror and compares the portraits to her image. Another technique is to have the patients touch their bodies. According to Dr. Weiss, "Most women avoid touching themselves, and many are amazed at their shape and size." With these techniques, women are able to develop a more realistic view of their bodies.

Visualization is also used to motivate people to stick to a diet plan. It's easier to work toward a goal if you are able to visualize yourself reaching that goal. Patients imagine what it will be like to fit into a pair of pants that are just a little too tight, and continually visualize new goals when they reach the old ones.

Another method of finding the causes behind people's dislike of their own bodies is to have the patients draw themselves at different times in their lives. The therapist can get a good idea of when the person first started to dislike him- or herself.

These feelings of dislike are often deeply ingrained emotional responses, and it can take a long time to change them and develop a new view of oneself. But techniques like mirroring and visualization can help people to be less obsessed with their bodies and better able to work toward attaining the weight and shape they desire.

Support Groups

Even when a program is successful at taking weight off, keeping it off is often a lifelong struggle. Many find Overeaters Anonymous is just the thing they need to keep them from falling off the wagon and gaining weight back. Some join OA as a last resort. Founded in 1960, Overeaters Anonymous holds nine thousand meetings each week in church

basements, hospitals, and community centers
around the country. It doesn't charge dues, it
doesn't advertise, and it doesn't offer diet recipes.
It is modeled after Alcoholics Anonymous, and its
goal is abstinence. However, "abstinence" in this
case is not abstinence from food as it is for alcohol
for members of AA; rather, it means abstinence
from abnormal eating patterns. Members are urged
to work out a personalized food program, often
with the help of veteran members. There are OA
meetings for teens that focus on their special inter-
ests and needs. However, OA is not for everyone.
Some are offended by its emphasis on surrendering
to a higher authority, which some see as God and
others take to mean whatever they want it to.

For some overweight people, getting help comes
in the form of learning to accept themselves as they
are. NAAFA, the National Association to Advance
Fat Acceptance, helps its members to feel good
about themselves. The group believes that if overweight people lose weight and become thinner
that's fine, but if they don't that's okay too. The
group also works to combat prejudice against fat
people in jobs, health care, and daily living.

MORE WEIGHT-LOSS AIDS

FOR MOST PEOPLE, the best way to lose weight is to combine dieting with exercise. But for many, such a scheme just doesn't work out. It takes a great deal of willpower to stick with a diet in the face of the constant temptations. Many overweight people find the idea of exercising regularly, day after day, even less appealing. They may have been inactive for years, and their extra weight has been taking its toll on muscles and joints. Now, physical activity—vigorous enough to burn off calories—is not only difficult; it hurts! Progress is very slow, too, with discouraging plateaus as the body adjusts to new metabolic patterns.

It's not surprising that millions are lured by schemes that promise quick weight loss without effort. One scheme, for instance, claimed that one could lose weight while sleeping. No exercising or dieting was necessary. Just take their Dream Away pills and your pounds would float away. Fortunately for the consumer, the Federal Trade Commission soon put a stop to that one. Another series of ads promised an amazing new "fat magnet," a weight-loss pill said to have been perfected by two "prominent doctors." The ads "guaranteed" a weight loss for anyone who took their pills—eat all you want, and the pounds will fall away "from the very first day." Popular columnist Ann Landers has answered questions about this and similar ads in several of her columns. Her opinion, backed by consultations with experts, is that in general, "If it sounds too good to be true, it probably is."

There are some aids and gimmicks on the market that do work—or at least help—in the struggle against excess pounds.

"No-Calorie Foods"

Diet drinks and low-calorie sweetners can be an aid to weight control, if the dieter uses them wisely. That means that they should be substituted for some other drink or food that is higher in calories and not used as an excuse to splurge on a rich dessert. But remember that a diet soda, for example, may help to quench your thirst and fill your stomach temporarily, but it does not contribute any useful nutrients. Even when you are trying to lose weight, you still need fuel for your body and a steady supply of vitamins and minerals.

Artificial sweetners can help to satisfy a dieter's sweet tooth, but for most obese people the main problem is not sugar but fat. Proctor & Gamble has developed a no-calorie fat substitute, *olestra*, now being reviewed by the FDA. Olestra is a sucrose polyester, a combination of the sugar sucrose with fatty acids.

The development of olestra was a sort of fortunate accident. The company's scientists had been looking for a new, easily digested fat that could be added to foods. Instead, they came up with one that could not be digested at all. The body got rid of it, unchanged. At first the researchers were very disappointed at their failure; then they realized that they had a wonderful dieting aid. Olestra could be added to foods, giving them the rich flavor typical of fats without adding any calories! (It has no cholesterol, either, and the body cannot convert it to cholesterol because it is not absorbed into the bloodstream. Instead, olestra actually lowers blood cholesterol by transporting the natural substance out of the body.)

Olestra is not intended to be a substitute for *all* the fat in the diet. People need a certain amount of fat to stay healthy. But it can replace about a third of the fat in oils and shortening used in cooking at home and three quarters of the fat used in restaurants and in snack foods such as potato chips. With olestra, the calorie count of a serving of french fries, for example, can be cut from 325 to 215.

Olestra still has not been approved by the FDA for use in foods, but other fat substitutes are already on the market. Nutra-Sweet's Simplesse is a mixture of proteins extracted from egg whites and skim milk, processed into microscopic globules that have a "mouthfeel" similar to fat. Simplesse can be used only in uncooked foods such as ice cream and salad dressing, because it loses its fatlike properties when heated. But Kraft Foods has come out with a whole line of "fat-free" foods from ice cream to baked goods. The effect of fat is simulated in these products by specially processed skim milk, egg whites, and cellulose gel, a dietary fiber.

Fooling the Appetite Centers

Most people who are overweight say they like the smell and taste of food. In fact, studies have shown that overweight people are much more influenced by taste in their eating habits than are people of normal weight. Susan Schiffman, a psychology professor at Duke University, theorized that perhaps food cravings could be partly satisfied by just enjoying food aromas. (Smell is actually an important part of what we call "taste." Think about your last head cold, when your nose was stuffed up and all your food tasted "blah.") Dr. Schiffman has come up with *Flavor Sprays*: tubes that contain one of an assortment of flavors: chocolate, strawberry, blueberry cheesecake, and many more. When an urge to eat too much seems overpowering, the overweight person merely sprays some Flavor Spray into his or her nose or mouth. After a few squirts of Flavor Spray, according to Dr. Schiffman, the body says "enough!"

Many diet experts are skeptical about using Flavor Sprays as a cure-all for weight loss. Dr. Schiffman agrees. "This is not a diet," she says. "It is a support for a diet. There is no way you're going to lose weight without cutting back on calories and, hopefully, exercising and doing all the responsible things."

Many powders and pills contain various forms of vegetable fiber, which absorbs great amounts of water and swells up in the stomach. The satiety center in the brain receives sensations of fullness and sends out messages to turn off the eating urge. This seems like an effective way of tricking the body into being satisfied with less food. The fiber itself has no calories because it is not digested. But as soon as the fiber leaves the stomach, the hungry feeling comes back. The "full" feeling lasts only for about thirty minutes to an hour.

Isn't there any "magic bullet" on the weight-loss scene? Not yet. Scientists at MIT were so enthusiastic about the amino acid tryptophan that they took out a patent for its use in weight loss. For many overweight people, tryptophan can dampen hunger pangs and permit them to skip that extra helping. But the future of this weight-loss aid is currently clouded by its possible link with eosinophilia-myalgia syndrome, a rare and sometimes fatal blood disease.

Tryptophan is a natural substance—indeed, an essential part of a normal diet (although not in such high doses). A variety of drugs have also been used as appetite suppressants to aid in weight-loss programs. The problem is that most drugs have undesirable side effects.

The over-the-counter drug phenylpropanolamine (PPA) is a prime example. It suppresses the appetite by blocking the hunger signals to the brain and also by drying the mouth, making foods taste bland and uninteresting. PPA's potentially dangerous side effects, mentioned in Chapter 8, have prompted some experts to urge that it be made available by prescription only; yet it is probably used more than any other drug by weight watchers today. Does it work? For some people, it does.

Another drug, *benzocaine*, is used in the form of chewing gum and candies. Benzocaine is a local anesthetic; it suppresses the appetite by numbing the taste buds that pick up sweetness. Taken before a meal, benzocaine diet aids make sweet foods less appetizing, but the dieter still has a taste for fats.

The drug is also used in the form of tablets that act in the intestine, putting the cells that send hunger signals to the brain to sleep for a while. The FDA says they work.

More powerful appetite-suppressing drugs are available. *Amphetamines*, for example, have been used for years to suppress appetite. These prescription drugs can be dangerous. One can easily become addicted to them, needing higher and higher doses to get the same effect. Amphetamines also produce feelings of euphoria and are often abused by people looking for a "high." In large doses they can harm the body. For these reasons, most states have banned their use for appetite control.

Recently, *Prozac*, a drug that has been widely used to treat depressed patients, has been found to cause weight loss. Its appetite-suppressing properties came to light by accident, when doctors noticed that depressed patients taking Prozac lost a great deal of weight. Eli Lilly, the company that makes the drug, is now testing it on hundreds of patients to find out just how effective it is as a weight reducer.

During the past twenty-five years, more than

fifty million people in over ninety countries have used a drug called *fenfluramine*. (It has been sold in the United States for more than twenty years under the name of Pondimin.) It is classified as an *anorectic*, a chemical that reduces the appetite. It is also a *thermogenic agent*—that is, it speeds up the rate at which the body burns food; one can eat normally and still lose weight. Pondimin works by stimulating cells in the brain to produce more serotonin. This is a chemical that has many effects, influencing appetite, mood, sleep, sexual behavior, and sensation. The problem with fenfluramine is that it has some undesirable side effects. Some people find their mouth is always dry. Others suffer from nausea or diarrhea. But someone who is extremely overweight may feel that losing weight is worth a little temporary suffering.

A newer version of this drug, called *dextrofenfluramine* (brand name Isomeride) has far fewer side effects and is even more potent than Pondimin in inducing weight loss. It has been used in Europe for years and may soon become available in the United States.

An adrenal hormone called *dihydroepiandrosterone (DHEA)*, is currently regarded as a promising thermogenic. Studies suggest that it not only burns off fat but promotes its replacement with muscle tissue. These effects occur without dieting or exercise, but the hormone has some drawbacks as a diet drug. It converts stored fat and cholesterol to estrogen, a female sex hormone that could have feminizing effects on men. Women taking DHEA might be bothered by the more masculine appearance resulting from the increase in muscle mass. Researchers are trying to synthesize variations of DHEA without these side effects.

A different kind of new weight-loss drug came out of studies of hibernating animals. Zoologist Albert Meier of Lousiana State University believes that people get fat because of body rhythms similar to those that store fat in animals preparing for hibernation or migration. He found that tiny doses of the drug *bromocriptine* decrease the secretion of the hormone prolactin, which promotes fat production in the liver. People who took the drug in experimental studies lost an average of 5 percent of their weight. Only fat was lost, no water, protein, or carbohydrates.

Drugs are far from an ideal way of losing weight, however. Nearly all drugs, no matter how "safe" they may be, have side effects that are bothersome or annoying. These range from a dry mouth to blurring of the eyes, headaches, diarrhea, constipation, stomach upset, and nervousness, as well as more serious problems. But that is not all. In just about all cases, once an obese person stops taking the drug, he or she gains back the weight that was lost.

Nonetheless, scientists keep searching for new and better drugs. Many different chemicals are now being investigated for possible weight-reducing properties. Judith Wurtman, a nutritionist at MIT and a leader in the field, believes that no one drug will solve all the problems of weight reduction. That thought is echoed by John Arch, a researcher at Beecham Pharmaceuticals in England, who says, "No one thinks drugs will ever cure obesity, or even replace dieting. But we can certainly improve on what we've got now."

Surgery

Struggling with the deprivations of dieting, the chores of exercising, or the annoying side effects of weight-loss drugs, many obese people must sigh now and then, and think, "If only I could just go to a doctor and have all this extra fat cut out!" That's not as farfetched as it sounds. Doctors today are using a number of surgical approaches to get rid of unwanted flab.

One of the quickest ways to remove fat from the body is by *liposuction*. A surgeon makes a tiny hole through the skin and slips in a long metal device that sucks out millions of fat cells located just under the skin. Each year hundreds of thousands of Americans have this operation. It has been used in the United States since 1982 and is now the leading form of cosmetic surgery. But that is all it is. To remove more than two to five pounds of fat during this operation would be dangerous, since much blood and body fluids are lost during the operation. So liposuction is NOT a technique for reducing.

What good is it, then? Liposuction can remove unsightly fatty bulges in most parts of the body: thighs, chin, buttocks, abdomen, knees, neck. Doctors can even reuse the fat cells that have been removed, cleaning them and injecting them to repair scars and fill in wrinkles and acne pits. Some doctors have even used a woman's own fat cells to enlarge her breasts.

But liposuction offers little hope for the obese. As Simon Fredricks, a plastic surgeon, says, "Liposuction is an operation of inches, not pounds." So the obese person must look elsewhere for help in losing weight.

In the 1970s surgeons tried some rather severe operations to help those who were "morbidly obese," that is more than a hundred pounds over the normal weight, or more than twice their ideal weight. One approach was the *small-intestine bypass.* Part of the person's small intestine was removed or rechanneled, so that no food could enter it.

The patients lost weight, all right. The small intestine is where most food digestion takes place, and also where most of the digested food is absorbed into the body. Unfortunately, the bypass operation was often accompanied by such severe complications that doctors abandoned the method.

Today, many thousands of severely obese people have parts of their stomach *stapled.* This cuts down on the amount of space in the stomach. There are two different ways a surgeon can do this. In the *gastric bypass*, metal staples are used to narrow the stomach to just a small pouch, through which the food can pass. In the operation called *gastroplasty*, the surgeon uses staples to guide the pathway food can take as it passes through the stomach. Each surgical method has its advantages. Since the stomach is now much smaller than normal, there is little room for the food one might eat. So the patient feels full after eating just a few bites. This has worked wonders for many people. Losses of fifty pounds or more are quite common with stomach stapling.

James Brolin, who has performed hundreds of these operations, spoke of one his patients who weighed 592 pounds. "This guy was at death's door." In eighteen months after the surgery, the patient lost 342 pounds! "But," warns Dr. Brolin, "stomach stapling should be considered a last resort. You should not consider surgery until all other methods fail." Dr. Brolin claims an 80-percent success rate for his operations. That is extraordinarily high, considering that most morbidly obese people will not succeed in losing weight and keeping it off over a long period of time, using the standard techniques of dieting and exercise.

Dr. Brolin, unlike many other doctors who merely staple off parts of the stomach, also closes off a small part of the small intestine. For reasons he does not understand, many of his patients find that they lose their desire for milk, milk products, and sweets. "All we know is that physiologically these foods do not taste good anymore to many of our patients."

Doctors have found that after surgery the amount of food necessary to make a person feel full is greatly reduced. Interestingly, most obese people skip breakfast. But they make up for it by gorging during most of the rest of the day. After surgery, however, even while the patients are losing up to a hundred pounds or more, they eat breakfast regularly.

Doctors have found that other things happen to obese patients after surgery. They feel better about themselves. Their spirits are higher than ever before. They get along with people much more easily. And they are much more active than they have been in years. Compare this with morbidly obese people who have lost weight through dieting or other means: They usually feel miserable, depressed, irritable, and anxious. They are constantly thinking about food. And almost always, they gain back the pounds they have lost with so much difficulty.

It would appear that surgery would be the best and surest way to lose weight. Many doctors agree, but they also say that only the morbidly obese should do it. It is, after all, a major operation and can be dangerous in a small number of cases. As more patients try surgery on the stomach, many different kinds of side effects are popping up. Most doctors agree we will need more time to find out about the long-term effects of these operations. But morbid obesity kills, and many of these people don't have the time to wait for final results.

For a while, in the 1980s, it looked as though doctors had come up with a simple, safe, and effective way for patients to lose weight. A plastic *gastric bubble* was placed in the stomach (by moving it through the mouth and down the esophagus). Once the plastic device was in the stomach, air was introduced and it swelled up to the size of a small juice can. It was thought that the bubble would help the patient to feel full after eating much smaller meals. After enough weight had been lost, the bubble could be removed, using an endoscope (a long, tubelike instrument designed to transmit images and perform manipulations inside a body organ or cavity). Early reports were exciting: People with a gastric bubble lost weight, with little discomfort. Later, however, as more people used it, complications set in. After a few months the bubble often lost its air and slipped through the stomach into the small intestine, where it got stuck. Then an operation was sometimes necessary to remove it. In other people, the constant rubbing of the balloon against the stomach wall caused a stomach ulcer, which began to bleed. In addition, some studies suggested that the diet counseling given to the patients was contributing more to their weight loss than was the bubble itself. Now, fewer doctors use this device.

Dentists are helping many obese people to lose weight. A device called the *Weight-Guard* is wired into place and makes it nearly impossible to open one's mouth wide. The person is forced to eat small bits of food, slowly. Many thousands have lost twenty to twenty-five pounds within a few months using this device. The problem is that in most cases, when the wire is removed, the obese-prone person regains just about all the weight that was lost.

Applied Psychology

Various techniques of behavior modification were described in the last chapter. They have had varying degrees of success, but for many people the painstaking effort needed to change long-established habits can seem too much like work.

Bringing your weight under control does take work and a lot of long-term dedication, but Maria Simonson, of Johns Hopkins University, may have found a helpful shortcut. Studying the eating habits of hundreds of people, she found that about 40 percent of them chewed their food more and ate less when they ate in a room painted light blue or light green. More than half of a group of dieters found that they lost more weight, more consistently, when they painted their kitchens or dining rooms blue or green. Red, yellow, and orange, on the other hand, were appetite stimulators. Fast-food restaurants typically use these colors, and so do Italian and Chinese restaurants. Howard Johnson

restaurants discovered that customers ate 134 percent more food when orange accents were added to
their blue dining rooms. So if you want to lose
weight, why not try redecorating—repaint your
kitchen blue or green.

ANOREXIA
NERVOSA

MILLIONS OF AMERICANS, especially teenagers and young adults, are risking their lives to be thin. Most of those in danger are females. To be "stylish," they are dieting and obsessively watching their waistlines.

Countless ads and TV commercials deliver the message that thin is beautiful. When a teenager or young woman begins a diet to attain this goal, though, the end result may be tragic.

The dieter, after achieving her original goal of losing a certain number of pounds, decides that just a few more pounds lost would be even better. Each day, as she looks at herself in the mirror, she is disappointed. "I'm still too fat!"

Her friends tell her, "You're getting as thin as a skeleton!" But the dieter, looking in the mirror, sees an image of herself that is distorted. Something has happened to her ability to judge herself and her own body. She has a disease called anorexia nervosa.

When Dieting Becomes a Disease

Anorexia nervosa is not a new disease. Doctors in Europe and America knew about it in the nineteenth century, but before World War II, anorexia was rare. Then in the 1960s, British fashion model Twiggy made being thin very stylish. From then on, if you were fat you were out, but thin was in.

Millions of women began to diet as never before, and young girls followed the fashion as well. One study showed that four out of five fourth-grade girls were dieting. According to another study, 20 percent of college women now have eating disorders, and anorexia nervosa is on top of the list.

Even famous people, those who have money and are the envy of millions, suffer from the disease.

Movie star Ally Sheedy and singer Pat Boone's daughter, Cherry, have both been through this terrible experience. One of the great singers of the 1970s, Karen Carpenter, died as a result of complications caused by anorexia nervosa.

Although no one is certain just how many people suffer from anorexia nervosa, most doctors agree the number is well over one hundred thousand. Most of them are girls and young women between the ages of fifteen and thirty, but growing numbers of men seem to be catching the thinness mania, and doctors are worried about an increasing trend of anorexia in the elderly. It used to be thought that anorexia nervosa and other eating disorders were mainly a problem of the well-to-do; more recent studies, however, show that the disease is spread among all social and economic levels, and it occurs among virtually all racial and ethnic groups.

What causes anorexia nervosa? Certainly our cultural emphasis on thinness is a contributing factor, but for most people dieting does not become an obsession. Athletic coaches may unintentionally contribute to the anorexic mindset by stressing programs of diet and physical activity designed to increase the proportion of lean muscle tissue and reduce fat. Ballet, a form of dance that requires a peak of physical fitness, has also produced far higher than average numbers of anorexics. Yet most people who take part in competitive athletics or ballet find the training a healthful experience. There is some evidence that eating disorders may run in families, but the findings are still preliminary and it is not certain whether the conditions are hereditary. Family dynamics seem to play an important role in the making of an anorexic, and so, too, do individual personality factors.

Portrait of the Anorexic

Experts don't know yet whether particular traits make it more likely that a person will become anorexic or whether they are traits that develop as the disease progresses. But they find that many anorexics have a great deal in common.

Often they are perfectionists. They insist that things be done just right. This emphasis on perfection may have developed as the result of pressures imposed by their parents. Many anorexics have a parent who tries to tell them what to do, all the time. They are not allowed to make up their own minds about what they will do with their lives. Often the anorexic's parents may seem like dictators, telling her who her friends must be, what she can read, or where she is allowed to go. For a teenager this can be very trying, but the anorexic usually does not rebel. The parents may brag about how "nice" their child is.

Anorexics may feel they have no control over their lives. Their parents dominate everything. So they rebel in a more subtle way: By forcing themselves to miss meals, they regain some control over their lives.

Food may be on their minds constantly; they may be hungry all the time. But by saying "No!" they gain a feeling of power. Doctors now have learned that anorexics gain something else, as well. They actually feel "high" for much of the time. When they starve themselves, the body reacts by releasing endorphins, the natural painkillers that act as messengers among the nerve cells in the brain and produce feelings of well-being.

Anorexics pay a huge price for their "highs."

First, of course, there is the great loss of weight.

Anorexics often lose more than 25 percent of their weight, some as much as 50 percent! A hundred-pound teenager who dieted her way into anorexia might drop down as low as fifty pounds. Many anorexics look like survivors of a World War II concentration camp.

A teenager who has already begun to have her periods will soon stop menstruating as anorexia progresses. Apparently the female body needs a certain level of body fat—enough to nourish a child that might be conceived—for the menstrual cycle to continue. If the monthly cycle has not yet started when the severe weight loss begins, the start of menstruation can be delayed for years. The anorexic's body stops developing; physically she remains a preadolescent girl.

Many anorexics find it difficult to sleep. They become irritable and lose their tempers easily. Depression often sets in as well. This causes them to avoid their friends, and they tend to stay at home. Their body temperature may drop, so that they feel cold all the time. They may spend a lot of time in bed because they are just too tired to move about.

But many anorexics spend time outdoors—running! They find that the activity burns calories and helps to keep their weight down; and the extra endorphins help to prolong the "high." In fact, doctors have now coined a special term for the condition in athletes who use running or other intense physical activity to cut down weight beyond the sensible limits of good health. They call it *anorexia athletica*.

The constant thoughts of food and eating (or not eating) make anorexics obsessed with their weight, and they typically check the scale several times a day. No matter what the scale shows, though, they are never satisfied. "My hips are too wide!" they exclaim. Or "Look at my stomach! How awful!" Or "My breasts are too large!" Yet the image that they see as disgustingly fat often looks frighteningly thin to the rest of the world.

Many anorexics develop rituals—things they do every day. Focusing on these rituals helps them to keep from eating. They may chew a piece of bread for ten minutes before they allow themselves to swallow it. Or they may tap the tabletop a hundred times before permitting themselves to eat a pea.

Anorexics may do things to take their minds off eating altogether, like brushing their hair every fifteen minutes or listening to loud music for hours on end.

Anorexics often become rude and self-centered. By this time they don't mind the fact that they have lost their best friends—they just want to be alone and away from everyone. If someone won't accept their opinion on some subject, they become insulted and may storm off, vowing never to speak to that person again.

Anorexics may skip school, preferring to spend the hours alone. Their whole life-style changes as they center their complete attention on keeping up their dieting and daydreaming about various aspects of eating. They get so thin that lying down hurts—there is no fat to cushion their bodies as their bare bones press against the hard mattress. Taking a bath in a hard tub is agony, too. And they are so cold all the time! So they move around as much as they can to generate heat.

When they look at themselves in the mirror, it is as though they were in a trance. They do not see their hollowed-out eyes, their protruding bones, and their caved-in abdomen and chest. Somehow they do not notice that their skin has become dry and rough and changed in color. It is darker than normal, even purplish, and their fingernails look a deathly blue. Even their hands and feet may have a ghastly blue tinge. They look like they are starving to death—and they are! But in their own eyes they still seem too fat.

Even with the little food that is eaten, the anorexic often has trouble getting rid of wastes and becomes constipated. Laxatives seem to help (and lower the weight still more) but can dangerously unbalance the levels of body fluids and chemicals.

Most anorexics at this stage are no longer interested in the opposite sex. Thoughts of romance and marriage rarely come to mind.

They may still retain a sense of humor, though. When asked by a doctor if she had eaten breakfast, one teenager replied, "Of course I had my breakfast; I ate my Cheerio." Another answered, "I licked a postage stamp. It has less calories."

Anorexia is no laughing matter. It can kill.

Tests of anorexics show various kinds of heart problems and dangerous changes in blood pressure. EEGs show abnormal brain wave patterns, which may help to explain why these obsessive dieters cannot see themselves as others see them.

Many anorexics suffer from osteoporosis, a severe loss of calcium from their bones. The bones become brittle and break easily. In young girls, permanent damage may be done to the bones, even if the anorexia is successfully treated. Curvature of the spine and stress fractures in the long bones of the feet are an increasing problem among young female athletes and ballerinas who have a history of excessive dieting. The severe weight loss also causes wasting of muscles, which may permanently lose their normal function.

Anorexia nervosa also takes a terrible toll on the patient's family. Parents, concerned about their sick child, may give him or her extra attention while neglecting other children in the family. The other children may resent this apparent favoritism and become jealous, competing with the anorexic child for their parents' attention and perhaps developing behavioral problems of their own. Younger siblings might try to copy their older sister and begin dieting, too. Older siblings may make life miserable for the dieter in hundreds of small but painful ways. So instead of the needed help, the family may just provide the anorexic with more reasons to sink deeper into his or her private, escapist world.

Treating Anorexia Nervosa

What can be done to help the anorexic?

The first thing that is needed is to recognize the condition—the earlier, the better. The sooner treatment is started, the simpler the solution. By the time the abnormal eating patterns have become well established, they may be very hard to correct.

How can parents, or siblings, or concerned friends tell if someone is becoming anorexic? With today's emphasis on thinness and fitness, it is sometimes hard to tell when "normal" dieting or running has crossed the line to a sickness.

Here are some danger signals to watch for:

- The person constantly thinks and talks about food or dieting.
- The diet never ends; as soon as one weight goal is reached, a new, lower one is set.
- The person is dieting secretly or lies about eating—for example, refuses a meal saying he or she ate at a friend's house.

- The person continually criticizes his
or her own appearance.

Treatment includes a combination of programs
for feeding the patient, psychological counseling,
and helping the patient to learn new behavior patterns. Sometimes drugs are used. Antidepressants
seem to help. The opiate blocker naltrexone has
also been used with good results. Hospital inpatient
programs can be very effective, providing a supportive environment in which psychological and
family problems can be worked on in addition to
supervised nutritional therapy.

In the feeding program it is important to get a
steady but moderate weight gain. If the weight gain
is too rapid, it may upset the patient, who may then
become uncooperative. Anorexics may lie and
cheat to keep on with their obsession on thinness.
Some obediently follow the eating program but
then sneak off to vomit up their meals in secret.
That was what happened to Karen Carpenter, who
was being treated for anorexia. She had been suffering from this condition for eight years, ever since
a review that called her "chubby" started her off on
a round of obsessive dieting. With therapy, she had

brought her weight back up to 108 pounds from a low of 83, but then the obsession with thinness returned and she began taking the drug ipecac after dinner each night, to make herself vomit. The chemical imbalances caused by repeated vomiting and the stress of the drug were too much for Karen Carpenter's heart and caused her death at the age of thirty-three.

Some anorexics only pretend to go along with the refeeding diet but instead drink ten glasses of water a day to fool the doctors with an apparent weight gain that is really only water. It becomes a game of wits between patient and doctor. Tests of body temperature show whether an anorexic is really progressing toward a more normal weight, but patients quickly learn to drink hot coffee or rub their hands over a light bulb before the test to raise their temperature.

The therapist may use a system of rewards, linking the return of certain privileges to increases in weight. For instance, anorexics may be allowed to leave the hospital for short periods or to do something they especially enjoy, as soon as their weight reaches a set target.

Psychological counseling is an important part of

the treatment, not only to motivate patients to cooperate with the feeding program but also to provide them with emotional support when their weight gain hits a plateau. When days or even weeks go by without a weight gain, even though the patient is really trying to get well, caring encouragement can help to get through the critical period.

The support of the family is also very important, not only at such critical times but during the whole treatment period. Every member of the family should play a role in the anorexic's recovery.

In cases where an anorexic is hospitalized, the average stay is six weeks. But therapy must continue long afterward. It is not unusual for therapy to continue for more than a year and sometimes up to three years.

About one half to two thirds of anorexics recover and can lead a normal life. But about a third of them will die or will be severely and permanently harmed by their experience.

For some it is a lifelong battle. As one former anorexic put it, "I have to cope with this every day. I try to figure out why I want to eat and why I want to starve."

BULIMIA NERVOSA

AT LAVISH BANQUETS in the later years of the Roman empire, the Roman nobles reclined on couches while slaves brought them huge, many-course meals of rich foods. If they were getting too full to appreciate the next course, they would leave to vomit out the food and drinks they had consumed, and then return to the dinner with an empty stomach, ready to eat again.

Today most people would consider that kind of behavior rather repulsive. Yet millions of American girls and young women periodically abuse themselves in a very similar way. After gorging on food—as much as 5,000 calories at a sitting—they sneak away to the bathroom and force themselves to vomit.

Why would anyone want to do that? They cannot help themselves. They feel compelled to go on periodic food binges, and then, consumed with guilt, they purge themselves either by vomiting or by taking strong laxatives. These unfortunate people are suffering from an illness called bulimia nervosa.

The Binge-Purge Disease

Bulimia nervosa has been known for many centuries, but in the past couple of decades it has exploded onto center stage. Although a small percentage of its victims are males, the overwhelming majority are females. An estimated 3 percent of women will be bulimic at some time in their lives; as many as 15 percent of college students periodically binge and purge. Eighteen is the average age for becoming bulimic.

The thinking patterns, attitudes, and beliefs of the bulimic are very similar to those of the anorexic. Many bulimics have previously had a history of anorexia nervosa, and about 50 percent of anorexics sometimes exhibit bulimic behavior—such as the purging that led to Karen Carpenter's death.

Both anorexia nervosa and bulimia nervosa are unfortunate results of our culture's emphasis on thinness. Adolescent girls and young women, perhaps already feeling a bit insecure because of the physical and emotional changes they have been experiencing, believe that the image they see when they look in the mirror does not match the accepted ideal of beauty. "I'm too fat," they sigh.

Yet there is so much tempting food around. Even social activities often involve eating—ice cream and cake at parties, buttered popcorn at the movies, hot dogs at the ball game, sharing a late-night pizza with friends at the dorm . . . Rejecting food would almost seem like rejecting life. For an insecure adolescent, it is also easy to get into the habit of eating when one is upset, taking comfort in sweet foods.

Fast foods, junk foods, party foods—all are chock-full of calories, many of them fat calories, just the thing to generate guilt for a modern girl or woman. If only she could undo the harm she just did by her uncontrolled eating! Throwing up, or taking a laxative so that the food will be rushed through her body unchanged instead of being turned into body fat, may seem like a logical solution. But then the food cravings strike again. In time the binge-purge pattern becomes a habit.

Some famous people have been bulimics. Among them are movie stars Ally Sheedy (who was also anorexic) and Jane Fonda, as well as Cathy Rigby, a former Olympic gymnast and now a TV sports commentator.

We are losing our war against bulimia nervosa. Each year the number of victims grows, and our success rate against this mysterious illness is discouragingly low. Yet most young people, faced with the same pressures and temptations, do not become obsessed with food and do not develop eating disorders such as anorexia or bulimia. Researchers are attempting to discover what makes the difference. What do bulimics have in common? What distinguishes them from the majority?

Portrait of the Bulimic

Spotting a bulimic is often very difficult. About three quarters of them are of normal weight, and most will do everything they can to hide their condition from everyone. But several times a week or even more often, they go on a food binge. They may "pig out" on cakes or pizzas or burgers or other rich foods, often stuffing them down at a breathless pace that may add up to 100 calories a minute. Then they make themselves vomit by sticking their fingers down their throats or taking an *emetic* drug (one that induces vomiting) such as ipecac. Some bulimics use laxatives in large-enough amounts to produce an almost constant diarrhea. The food is moved through the intestines so rapidly that very little of it is digested or absorbed.

After a time, vomiting up food may become a reflex, and no emetic or laxative will be needed. To make certain they keep the pounds off, many bulimics exercise strenuously every day. About one quarter of them are so successful in counteracting their huge calorie intake that they become ano-rexic. (Some specialists have suggested that in addition to anorexia and bulimia, a mixed problem—bularexia—should also be recognized.) As the bizarre life-style continues, the bulimic's fear of gaining weight grows and adds to the com-pulsion.

Attempts to help bulimics are hampered by the

fact that they do not hesitate to lie to cover up their condition. Because most of them look normal, they can fool family, friends, and even doctors.

There may be some telltale signs, however, that can point to the correct diagnosis.

A bulimic is often tired and suffers from weakness, due to the lack of calories absorbed by her body. The loss of fluids from continual vomiting or diarrhea disrupts the balance of body chemicals and leads to a variety of symptoms. Her hands and feet may swell. She may suffer from a bloated feeling or abdominal fullness. Headaches and nausea are common.

These are all rather general symptoms, though, that might be caused by a variety of ailments. But there are some more specific signs that an alert doctor may spot. The habit of continually putting fingers into the mouth to bring on vomiting may produce characteristic scars on the back of the bulimic's hands. Her salivary glands may be enlarged. And the acid gastric juices that she vomits up gradually wear away the enamel of her teeth. Many bulimics need a lot of dental work because of rotting teeth.

The frequent use of laxatives can cause heart

problems. The acid vomit, as well as the emetics or
laxatives, may also produce gastrointestinal problems.

A large number of bulimics suffer from other
compulsive behavior. In addition to the compulsion to continually binge and purge, they may
develop rituals, doing particular things over and
over. These rituals are often related to their bulimic
behavior.

Following a binge, a bulimic feels guilty and
helpless, with no control over her actions, and she
may become depressed. Bulimics are more likely to
take drugs such as marijuana or cocaine than non-
bulimics. They also get drunk or smoke more often
than others.

Bulimics may attempt suicide or be hospitalized for depression or other mental problems.
They are more likely to steal than most other
women. They also tend to suffer from menstrual
disorders and are given to mood swings in far
higher percentages than for other women their
age.

Despite all these problems, the bulimic often
will present a confident outward appearance—
friendly, competent, and seemingly in control of

her life. Inwardly, however, she is drowning in a sea of turmoil—angry, hurt, lonely, and needy. The bulimic's mood swings may alternate from a stubborn independence to a desperate need for love and affection.

What Causes It?

Why does a person become a bulimic? Although the causes are many, there is usually a common motive: a desire to become thin.

Modern attitudes feed this desire in two different ways, as we saw in Chapter 3. First, there is the idea that thin is beautiful. In addition, as women have entered traditional male fields, in business, politics, and other areas of life, some have translated the need to compete successfully into a need to look more like the male image—and men typically lack the soft, rounded contours of the well-nourished female body.

There are also family reasons. For some bulimics, their mothers served as their role models. If the mother was forever on a diet, it seemed only natural for the daughter to follow in her footsteps. Once started, the dieting got out of control.

Sometimes family problems were the factor that started the bulimic on her self-destructive way. She might have tried to be a mediator in a family dispute, or felt caught between two parents getting a divorce. Perhaps a parent was an alcoholic, or someone in the family was seriously ill, placing stresses on all the family members.

One study found that nearly half of all bulimics were sexually abused as children. Many children blame themselves for such abuse. The shame that follows is often translated into low self-esteem. They hate their bodies and try to purify themselves through fasting and excessive exercise.

Although psychological factors such as these may contribute, researchers have recently discovered that bulimia nervosa may have physical causes as well. Our growing knowledge about the nature of these physical factors may ultimately yield effective treatments.

Some scientists believe that something has gone wrong with the brain chemistry of bulimics. The mood centers and appetite centers in the hypothalamus seem to be vitally involved. The fact that bulimics have problems involving mood swings, stress, and foods appears to support this hypothesis. So, too, does the finding that bulimics do not respond normally to the brain chemical serotonin. It has been found that antidepressants that improve the efficiency of serotonin as a message carrier in the brain also relieve many of the symptoms of bulimics. Their mood swings are smoothed out, and they may lose their desire to binge and vomit.

Studies linking abnormal endorphin levels with bulimia nervosa were described in Chapter 7. Other studies have found that bulimics have a reduced supply of cholecystokinin (CCK), a hormone in the intestines that is normally secreted after a meal. As we saw in Chapter 6, CCK in the blood is a signal of "fullness" to the control centers in the hypothalamus. But a bulimic's CCK level is lower than normal, even after a meal; so the appetite-damping mechanism is not turned on, and the bulimic continues to eat. When bulimics are given CCK, most of them stop or at least cut back on their binges. Another interesting finding is that when bulimics take antidepressants, after a couple of months their CCK levels become normal.

Treating Bulimia

The antidepressant Prozac, discussed in Chapter 12 as a weight-loss aid, seems to be very successful treatment for bulimics, too. Nearly all the patients observed ate less because "after a few bites they no longer feel the urge to eat," says Leslie Solyom, a Canadian psychiatrist who ran the study. Other doctors have made similar comments.

But many specialists in food disorders feel that drugs are not enough. They feel that a psychiatrist must work with the bulimic in an attempt to understand and perhaps resolve the underlying emotional causes of the problem. They note that when drugs are stopped, the bulimic usually returns to her habits of binging and purging.

The psychologist not only tries to find out the emotional causes of the problem but offers ways to change the bulimic's faulty eating patterns. Attempts are made to boost the patient's self-esteem. Often participation in group meetings is urged. When a bulimic discovers that others suffer from the same disorder and can hear them speak of their ordeal, it becomes easier to face and overcome her own problem. These techniques are actually rather similar to those used successfully for decades with alcoholics.

For bulimics who are suffering from severe depression, suicidal feelings, or substance abuse, inpatient treatment in a supportive hospital setting may be necessary.

As a person recovers from bulimia nervosa, many adjustments must be made. Wherever possible, the damage to her body must be repaired. (In some cases the damage may be so severe that complete recovery is not possible.) The recovery period can be a difficult time: daily battles with hunger, bloating, and aches and pains throughout the body due to the long years of abuse.

The recovering bulimic must learn to detach herself from some of her concern about family problems and get more involved with her peers. She must view her body differently. She must learn to respect herself more as a human being. Some psychiatrists use techniques of visualization, having the bulimic create a positive mental image of herself.

Often the entire family is invited to attend therapy sessions, at which problems are aired out. This can be very painful for all involved. Frequently, however, many long-standing problems are resolved in these sessions. At the very least, all the family members see things they may not have been aware of and can take positive actions.

A very detailed eating program is often suggested. The support of other bulimics can be very helpful in providing motivation to stick to the program. Such groups as Overeaters Anonymous and the American Anorexia/Bulimia Association sponsor regular meetings for this purpose.

Despite the combined use of psychiatric treatments and drugs, bulimia nervosa remains a stubborn problem. One study showed that the majority of bulimics were unimproved after two years of treatment. Another study found that after treatment one third are cured, another third will improve, but fully one third of bulimics will not be helped at all.

It is clear that much remains to be done in this field. Research into the biochemistry of the brain is gradually yielding new insights and more effective treatments. But it seems unlikely that the terrible toll of eating disorders such as anorexia nervosa and bulimia nervosa will be reduced unless there are some drastic changes in our social values. The emphasis on thinness (and more recently on a "fit" appearance) is only a part of a broader attitude. We tend too much to judge people on the basis of appearance, setting the ideals for both women and men on superficial qualities rather than the deeper traits of personality, intelligence, and character. As long as people are viewed as sex objects rather than valuable and unique individuals, some will accept these superficial standards as the measure of their own worth and become obsessed with the need to match the "ideal."

The women's movement has attempted to bring about just such a revolution of values. They have made some progress, but there is a long way to go. The fact that an estimated 2 percent of American girls and women have developed anorexia nervosa, another 3 percent are bulimic, and their numbers are growing, is a symptom of a much broader sickness in our society. Its cure will take the cooperation of advertisers, moviemakers, and a wide range of other creative people.

MAINTAINING THE RIGHT WEIGHT FOR *YOU*

ONCE AN OVERWEIGHT person has lost weight, or an anorexic has gained weight, or a bulimic has stabilized his or her weight, the battle still isn't over. The key is to maintain that weight for the rest of one's life. The only way to do this is to learn new, healthier eating habits.

Perhaps the most important part in this change of habits is moderation. Once you've reached your desired weight, don't eat too much, or too little. It's all right to eat most foods, but avoid fatty foods as much as possible, and try not to eat too much of anything at once. As one doctor tells his patients, it's all right to eat anything, but not everything.

It won't be easy to stick to a change in life-style,

but if you go back to your old habits you'll go back to your old weight. A certain amount of self-denial is inevitable. But substituting healthier foods for unhealthy ones doesn't mean that the new diet has to consist of seaweed and vitamins. Just choose food wisely—fish and chicken instead of beef and pork, for example; whole-grain foods with fiber instead of processed foods; fruits and vegetables instead of sugar snacks; low-fat milk and dairy products instead of fatty ones; water or juice instead of soda—these are the types of substitutions that many people find they enjoy more than fat-laden diets, once they've changed their eating habits.

Of course, exercise must accompany any change in life-style. A daily routine each day, doing something you enjoy, is the best idea; but even if it's just walking after dinner, taking the stairs instead of the elevator, mowing the lawn with a push mower instead of an electric riding mower, or working in the garden—any way you can keep your body moving will help you stay in shape, feel better, and maintain your new weight.

Another important barrier to overcome is to realize that many compulsive eating problems arise from psychological needs. Learn to fulfill these needs with hobbies that you enjoy. They will give you satisfaction in addition to keeping you busy and keeping your mind off food.

Some doctors suggest you continue to weigh yourself regularly. If your weight goes over your target, try a little harder to avoid temptations, then relax a little when you return to your target weight.

Last, but not least, learn to feel good about your body and yourself. With improved body image and self-image, you'll learn to take better care of your body, and it will take better care of you.

FURTHER READING

Angier, Natalie. "Fat on Thighs and Paunches Is the Fate of All Mammals," *The New York Times*, October 30, 1990, pp. C1–C2.

Long, Patricia. "Kids With a Lot to Lose," *Hippocrates*, November/December 1988, pp. 70–78.

Longstreet, Dana. "Make Friends With Your Body," *American Health*, July/August 1988, pp. 72–75.

Miller, Annetta, et al. "Diets Incorporated," *Newsweek*, September 11, 1989, pp. 56–62.

Moll, Lucy. "Poundwise: Rev Up," *Health*, June 1989, pp. 45–46.

Stoffel, Jennifer. "What's New in Weight Control," *The New York Times*, November 26, 1989, p. 17.

Toufexis, Anastasia. "Dieting: The Losing Game," *Time*, January 20, 1986, pp. 54–60.

Wooley, Susan, and O. Wayne. "Thinness Mania," *American Health*, October 1986, pp. 68–74.

Zarrow, Susan, ed. "Good, Better, Best Weight-Loss Ideas for 1988," *Prevention*, January 1988, pp. 34–41, 118–123.

Abraham, Suzanne, and Derek Llewellyn-Jones. *Eating Disorders: The Facts*, Oxford: Oxford University Press, 1984.

Brown, Laura, and Esther Rothblum. *Overcoming Fear of Fat*, Binghamton, New York: Harrington Park, 1989.

Hollis, Judi. *Fat Is a Family Affair*, Center City, Minnesota: Hazelden, 1985.

Kolodny, Nancy J. *When Food's a Foe*, Boston: Little, Brown, 1987.

Lansky, Vicki. *Fat-Proofing Your Children*, New York: Bantam, 1988.

Levenkron, Steven. *The Best Little Girl in the World*, New York: Warner, 1978.

INDEX

adipose cells. *See* fat cells.
adipsin, 72
adrenaline, 64
aerobic capacity, 136
aerobic exercise, 135
AIDS, 68
alpha$_2$ receptors, 76–77
American Anorexia/
    Bulimia Association,
    201
American Heart Association,
    10
amino acids, 44
ammonia, 46
amphetamines, 163
Andres, Reubin, 10
anorectic drugs, 164
anorexia athletica, 181

anorexia nervosa 4, 15, 21,
    82–85, 175–88
    characteristics of, 178–84
    diagnosis, 185–86
    treatment, 186–88
appetite, 67–72, 88, 131, 134
appetite suppressants,
    162–64
Arch, John, 166
artificial sweeteners, 158
ascorbic acid, 47

ballet, 178
basal metabolic rate
    (BMR), 51, 61, 62,
    64, 101, 116
beauty, ideals of, 17–20,
    25–28, 202

behavior modification,
    146–48
benzocaine, 162–63
beta₁ receptors, 76–77
bicycling, 130
binge-purge disease. *See*
    bulimia.
Blass, Elliott, 81
blood sugar level, 69
Bogardus, Clifton, 62
body fat, 11–14, 53
    distribution of, 36–37, 77
body image, 16, 21, 196.
    See also self-image.
body mass index (BMI), 14
Boone, Cherry, 177
Brolin, James, 169–70
bromocriptine, 165
Brownell, Kelly, 98–101
Brunzell, John, 103
bularexia, 193
bulimia nervosa, 4, 15, 21,
    80, 189–202
    characteristics of 190–96
    diagnosis of 192–96
    treatment 199–202
bulimics. *See* bulimia.

calorie, 50, 122
    counts, 50, 53, 57, 107,
        115, 129–30
    requirements, 110–11
Calorie, 49

cancer, 33, 68
carbohydrates, 42–43, 52,
    87, 88–89, 102, 106
cravers, 89
cardiovascular disease,
    31–33, 102
Carpenter, Karen, 177,
    186–87, 191
cholecystokinin (CCK), 72,
    198
cholesterol, 31, 33, 37
clean plate syndrome, 121,
    122
color, effects on appetite,
    173–74
compulsive behavior, 195
cross-addiction, 85
cycling (yo-yo dieting), 98

depression, 35, 89, 131, 195
dextrofenfluramine, 164
diabetes, 33, 34, 38
diet, definition of, 105
"dietary failure syndrome,"
    117
Diet Center, 149
diet centers, 148–49
Diet Cops, 145
diet diary, 109–10, 146
dieting, 92–103
    avoiding relapse after,
        118–23
    effects on brain of, 87

failure, 116–18
hazards of, 94–95
health risks of, 102, 145
planning of, 106–111
diet services 143
dihydroepiandrasterone
(DHEA), 164–65
Disney, Anthea, 26
Dopamine, 87
Dougherty, Darlene, 121
Drenick, Dr. Ernst, 7
drug abuse, 195

eating habits, 55, 204
electrical impedence test,
12
emetic drugs, 193
endorphins, 73, 81–87, 179,
181, 198
enzymes, 43
estrogens, 73
exercise, 78, 97, 124–40,
148, 204

fad diets, 145
Fallon, April, 20
families of anorexics, 184,
188
families of bulimics,
196–97, 200–1
Family Weight Loss
Centers, 149
"fast" muscle fibers, 133

fasting, 96, 150
fat cells, 40, 74–77
"fat phobia," 15
fats, 40–42, 52, 57, 75, 102,
106, 108–9, 165
fatty acids, 75, 76
fenfluramine, 164
fiber, 48, 161
fidgeting, 63
fitness, 125–29
Fitness and Body Fat
Analyzer, 13
flavor sprays, 160–61
fluoxetine, 89–90
Fonda, Jane, 192
food addiction, 71–91
food cravings, 87, 89,
119–20, 160
food diary, 109–10, 146
Food and Drug
Administration (FDA),
94
Ford Modeling Agency,
26
Fredericks, Simon, 168

gastric bubble, 171–72
gastric bypass, 169
gastroplasty, 169
Gibbs, James, 72
girth, 139–40
glycerol, 75, 76
Greene, Loren, 130

Gregory, Dick, 142
Gwinup, Grant, 130, 138

Harris, Louis, 126
Haskell, William, 124
heart attack, 31, 33
heart disease, 31
height-weight tables, 9–11
heredity, 133
    and obesity, 64–66, 103
high blood pressure, 32, 33,
    37
high-fiber diet, 107
Hirsch, Dr. Jules, 66
Hudson, Walter, 141–42
hunger center, 68
hydrostatic weighing test, 12
hypnosis 150–51
hypothalamus, 68, 197

ideal weight, maintenance
    of, 103–5
immune system, 34
insulin, 70–71, 134–35
ipecac, 187

Jenny Craig Weight-Loss
    Centers, 149
Jonas, Jeffrey, 82

Kempner's Rice Diet
    program, 151

Kern, Philip, 101
kilocalories, 50
knee bends, 138
Kroll, Joseph, 69
kwashiorkor, 45

laxatives, 183, 193
lean body mass, 11, 97
leg lifts, 138
Leibowitz, Sarah, 87
Levitsky, David, 134
Lieberman, Harris R., 89
lipoprotein lipase (LPL), 76,
    101–2
liposuction, 167–68
liquid diet programs,
    149–50
low-calorie foods, 157–60
low-density lipoproteins
    (LDLs), 102
low-impact aerobic
    exercises, 136, 137
Luby, Elliot, 82

Marlatt, Dr. Alan, 118
Marrazzi, Mary Ann, 82,
    85
Maxwell, Morton H., 144
Meier, Albert, 165
menstruation, 83, 84, 180,
    195
mental illness, 35

metabolism, 50, 99, 131–33,
    139
  brain, in eating disorders,
    88
  slowing with age, 123
Metropolitan Life Insurance
    Company, 9, 10
minerals, 47
mirroring, 152
mood swings, 198
morbid obesity, 8, 168, 171
morphine, 82, 85
muscles, 133
  tissue loss, 96–97

naloxone, 86
Naltrexone, 81, 84, 186
National Association to
    Advance Fat
    Acceptance (NAAFA),
    155
neuropeptide Y, 87, 88
New Jersey Law Against
    Discrimination, 25
norepinephrine, 87, 89
normal weight, 9, 10
Nutri/System programs, 149

obesity 1–2
  causes of, 54–78
  cultural influences on,
    55–56

definition of, 7–8
  environmental effects on,
    55–60
  health hazards of, 8,
    30–37
  and heredity, 64–66, 103
  morbid, 8, 168, 171
  significant, 8
olestra, 158–59
Optifast, 143, 149, 150
osteoporosis, 183–84
Overeaters Anonymous,
    154–55, 201
overeating, 21

phenylpropanolamine
    (PPA), 95, 162
Pima Indians, 63, 65
plateau, 100–1, 132
pleasure, 86
Pondimin, 164
prejudice against fat people,
    2–3, 23–25
Pritikin longevity centers,
    151
protein, 43–46, 52, 87, 102,
    106
Prozac, 163, 199
psychological counseling,
    151–54, 187–88,
    199–201
pulse rate, 135–36

purging. *See* laxatives,
    vomiting.
push-ups, 138

"refeeding," 150
residential programs, 150
Retton, Mary Lou, 152–53
rewards
    food, 59, 80
    nonfood, 147, 205
Rigby, Cathy, 192
rituals, 181, 195
Rozin, Paul, 20

satietin, 69
satiety center, 68
saturated fats, 41
Schiffman, Susan, 160
schizophrenia, 35
Schwartz, Joe, 127
sculpting, 152–53
sedentary life-style, 57–58,
    124–25
self-esteem, 21, 22, 147
self-image, 21, 74, 154,
    175–76, 183, 205
serotonin, 70, 88–89, 164,
    198
set point theory, 78
Shapiro, Leona, 74
Sheedy, Ally, 177, 192
Shepard, Roy K., 129
Shepherd, Cybill, 27

Simonson, Maria, 173
Simplesse, 159
sit-ups, 137–38
skinfold calipers, 12
"slow" muscle fibers, 133
small-intestine bypass, 168
Solyom, Leslie, 199
South America, 7
"spontaneous physical
    activity," 63
starches, 42
Stark, Robert E., 108, 109
statistics
    anorexia nervosa, 177,
        188
    bulimia nervosa, 190
    dieting, 8, 15, 126, 176
    eating disorders, 5, 176
    exercise, 125–27
    fitness, 57, 125
    obesity, 3, 7, 28, 65
    weight-loss programs,
        144–45
stomach stapling, 168–70
stress, 59–60, 82, 131
strokes, 32, 33
sugars, 42
support groups, 154
surgery, 166–73
swimming, 137, 138

Take Off Pounds Sensibly
    (TOPS), 149

television watching, 58, 125
thermic response, 113
thermogenesis, 61
thermogenic agents, 164–65
timing of meals, 111–13
tocopherol, 47
toe touches, 138
triglycerides, 31, 37
tryptophan, 71, 161–62
Turner, Kathleen, 27
Twiggy, 176
twins, identical, 66

ultrasound, 12
underweight condition, 16
unsaturated fats, 41

Van Itallie, Theodore, 59
visualization, 152–54
vitamins, 47–48
vomiting, 189–90, 193

walking, 130, 136
water, 48–49

water weight, 11, 116, 121, 137
weight, ideal, maintenance of, 103–5
Weight Cycling Program, 100
Weight-Guard, 172
weight loss, 53
    fraud, 157
    gimmicks, 94
    programs, 143–55
    rate, 106, 111, 148
Weight Watchers 148–49
Weigle, Scott, 131
Weiss, Fran 152–53
willpower, 156
Winfrey, Oprah, 149–50
Wooley, Susan C., 16
Wurtman, Judith, 89, 166
Wurtman, Richard, 69–71, 88, 89
wrestlers, 100

yo-yo dieting, 98–103